The Way We V
Bath

Bath has attracted famous and wealthy visitors for many centuries. They sought the curing waters and were part of the exclusive 'fashionable society'. When the Great Western Railway arrived in 1840, Bath was suddenly within easy reach of people living in towns and cities across the south of England and thousands of day trippers and holiday makers flocked to the city.

On arrival, they wanted to know what to see and where to go and guide-books were available to help them make the most of their stay.

This book combines text from a Bath guide published in 1917 with photographs from the same period.

It is remarkably detailed and includes chapters on how to get there; where to stay; local and social history; excursions by electric tram to places of interest; walks; famous residents and much more.

The original book, reproduced here, is over one hundred years old and not in the best condition. As a consequence, there are some marks, faded areas, dark patches and other blemishes on the pages of this book.

The photographs and illustrations within the body of the text are from the original guide-book and aren't the finest quality. Those at the end of the book are from glass, 'magic lantern' projection slides and are much sharper and clearer.

The text and photographs complement each other and enable us to travel back in time to one of England's most beautiful and culturally rich cities, over one hundred years ago. I hope you enjoy the journey.

Andrew Gill

INTRODUCTION.

Kit Marlowe : How likest Bath ?
Shakespeare : Like it, Coz ?
As turtle-billing lovers their ladies' lips !
A pearl and peerless pattern of all cities !
Hid 'mid its hills like Eve in Paradise,
It lacks no loveliness could tempt the soul—
Yet weeps no harm its waters may not heal.
Well may the tired sun couch him in the west
Whose fragrant bed distils such benison.

From *Episode V : Bath Pageant,* by Rev. W. P. Hanks.

Bath as a Health and Holiday Resort—Railway and Road Routes—Hotels and Tariffs.

THERE is in the aspect and situation of Bath a charm which not only appeals at once to the visitor, but is the constant joy and pride of those most familiar with it. The beautiful city in its quiet garb of soft grey, as it nestles amid the green of the encircling hills, presents an alluring picture of which the eye never tires. Towers and spires, groves and gardens, stately thoroughfares that have made their architects famous, historic memorials erected centuries ere the English nation was founded, surrounding hills and vales of exceeding beauty, combine to give Bath a proud position among the cities of our land.

Poets and novelists, essayists and historians, have enshrined the praises of Bath in enduring literature, and many of them have been happy in being numbered among its residents ; and the tablets affixed to historic houses show that there is scarcely a street in the city without association with some illustrious name.

There is an abiding charm in the tender browns and greys of the old stone-built city. Look down upon Bath from the crags of Beechen Cliff ; or stand upon the historic hill of Lansdown and let the eye travel towards the fringing willows of the valley along which the Avon steals in silver coils on its course towards the Channel, while tier over tier the lines of

INTRODUCTION

hills fade into the haze of the " Severn Sea " ; and then enjoy the prospect over the verdant landscape to the hill-embosomed city. Or, yet again, go to the greensward in front of the Royal Crescent—that magnificent sweep of houses in a subtly calculated combination of dignity and elegance—and from that stately vantage-point survey Bath with her background of hills ; and, whether the city is seen from Cliff, or Down, or Crescent, none can fail to offer a tribute to her peerless beauty.

Bath as a Health Resort.

Apart from the medicinal value of the Hot Springs, to which a section of this book is devoted, Bath has its value as a health resort, particularly to invalids in the winter time ; for the air is peculiarly sweet and fresh, and the encircling hills protect the city from cold winds ; while those who desire bracing air can find it on the slopes of Lansdown Hill and Combe Down, up which stretch long roads of pleasant residences. It is justly claimed that scarcely any other English town is graced with suburbs so bracing as these air-swept heights.

Bath as a Holiday Resort.

Thousands of visitors come to Bath neither to sip the waters, nor to wash in them, nor for any climatic reason ; but simply to spend a holiday amid the attractions of the city and neighbourhood. For them there are the Roman remains and the Abbey ; an endless round of amusements and varied interests in theatres, concerts, and band performances ; golf, tennis and cricket ; croquet and bowls ; boating and angling ; and an enchanted land of parks, gardens, and stately streets. In addition, the neighbourhood is rich in delightful walks, and all day long electric trams whiz passengers to outlying and uplying suburbs, from which again the walks are fresh and charming. Bristol, with the beauties of Clifton, is brought within easy distance by a fast and frequent train service ; and the holy ground of Glastonbury, the ancient and stately beauty of Wells, and the wonders of Cheddar Cliffs, may all be visited with ease.

RAILWAY ROUTES.

Access is provided by the Great Western and the Midland Companies, and by a combination of the Midland and the

RAIL AND ROAD ROUTES

London and South-Western Companies, who work the Somerset and Dorset Joint Line. The **Great Western** has its passenger station in Manvers Street, and the **Midland** at Green Park. The Midland terminus and offices serve also for the **Somerset and Dorset Line.** The stations of the two companies are about half a mile apart.

The fast trains, of which there is an excellent service, accomplish the journey from Paddington in two hours. **Single Fares** from Paddington, 17s. 10d. and 8s. 11d.; **Tourist Tickets**, available six months, 31s. 3d. first, 17s. third. **Week-End tickets,** 24s. and 12s.

Cheap Excursion Tickets to and from Bath are also frequently issued during the summer, particulars of which may be had from the time-tables and other announcements of the several companies. The usual return excursion fare for periods varying from four to fifteen days is 12s.

Among the many facilities offered by the enterprising Great Western Railway Company mention may be made of the **Circular Day Trips** run in summer, embracing Bath, Cheddar and Wells, at the low inclusive return fare from London of 7s., third class.

MOTOR AND CYCLE ROUTES.

From London.

From Hyde Park Corner take the Knightsbridge Road, and along Hammersmith Broadway to King Edward VII Bridge (6 miles). Do not cross the bridge, but keep straight on through Brentford to Hounslow, where keep to right at fork. The road is easily found by way of Longford and Colnbrook to **Slough** (20½ miles), and on to **Maidenhead** (26¼). Two miles farther on keep to left and through Twyford to **Reading** (39). The route is then by way of Calcot Green, Theale, and Thatcham to **Newbury** (56), Hungerford (64½), and **Marlborough** (74½). At end of Marlborough High Street bear left, then turn sharply to right, and to left at the College. On through Fyfield and West Kennet to **Beckhampton** (81 miles). From Beckhampton there is a choice of routes—the rather hilly direct road, and the easier road *via* Devizes, about 2½ miles longer than the former. The direct route, which we will follow, passes by way of Calne to **Chippenham** (93¼), where bear left after crossing the Avon, and ascend a rather steep hill. Having descended the hill, keep to right under railway arch and wheel through Pickwick, bearing to right just beyond old toll-house, and after a long, steady rise there is a pleasant run down to **Box** (100¼). At Bathford arch keep to right, and there is then no mistaking the road through Batheaston to **Bath** (106 miles).

N.B.—Those who take the longer but easier road from Beckhampton *via* **Devizes** and Melksham will join the direct Bath road at Box.

From the Midlands.

(The shorter but harder route.)

Birmingham is taken as a starting-point, for convenience ; motorists and cyclists in neighbouring towns will need no instruction how to adapt their own centres to the main route. The direct road from Birmingham is by way of Moseley, King's Heath, Studley, Alcester and **Evesham** (29¾), and on through Teddington to **Cheltenham** (45¾ miles). Then the route lies across a spur of the Cotswolds—very hard riding for miles—to **Stroud** (59½ miles), and *via* Nailsworth, Dunkirk, Cold Ashton and Swainswick to **Bath** (88¼ miles).

(The longer but much easier route.)

This route adds nearly 13 miles to the distance, but, as it is practically level the whole way, it is strongly recommended to cyclists. Proceed by way of King's Heath, Alcester and Evesham, as in the shorter route, to Cheltenham, and there branch off to **Gloucester** and on through Bristol to Bath.

HOTELS AND TARIFFS.

Hotels of all grades are numerous, as will be seen from the following list of the more important establishments, some of which rank with the best in England. The tariffs were supplied by the proprietors, but **owing to changes of management and other causes** it is always wise to verify these matters beforehand. Apartments are also readily obtained.

Where the hotel accommodation includes *Motor Garage* a note is made to that effect.

HOTELS AND TARIFFS

Bath.

Empire : *R.*, single, fr. 6/– ; double, fr. 10/– ; *b.* or *l.*, 3/6 ; *t.*, 1/– ; *d.*, 6/– ; *a.*, nil.
  Boarding terms : fr. 12/– per day ; fr. 84/– per week ; fr. 24/– per week-end. Garage.

Pulteney : *R.*, single, fr. 5/– ; double, fr. 9/– ; *b.*, 2/6 ; *l.*, 2/6 ; *t.*, 1/– ; *d.*, 5/– ; *a.*, nil.
  Boarding terms : fr. 73/6 per week. Motor Garage.

Lansdown Grove, Lansdown Road : *R.*, single, fr. 4/– ; double, fr. 6/6 ; *b.*, 2/6 ; *l.*, 2/6 ; *t.*, 1/– ; *d.*, 3/–.
  Boarding terms : fr. 10/6 per day ; fr. 73/6 per week. Garage.

York House : *R.*, single, 5/– ; double, fr. 7/6 ; *b.*, 2/6 ; *l.*, fr. 2/6 ; *t.*, 1/– ; *d.*, 5/–.
  Boarding terms : fr. 10/6 per day ; fr. 73/6 per week. Motor Garage.

Bath Hydro.

Christopher, High Street : *R.*, single, 2/6 ; double, 5/– ; *b.*, 2/6 ; *l.*, 3/6 ; *l.*, 1/– ; *d.*, 3/6 ; *a.*, 1/6.
  Boarding terms ; 10/– per day ; 63/– per week.

Royal Station, Railway Place : *R.*, single, 3/– ; double, 5/– ; *b.*, 2/6 ; *l.*, 2/6 ; *t.*, 2/6 ; *d.*, 4/– ; *a.*, 1/–.
  Boarding terms : 10/6 per day ; 63/– per week ; 21/– per week-end. Motor Garage.

Ralph's, opposite Midland Station : *R.*, single, 2/– ; double, 3/6 ; *b.*, fr. 1/3 ; *l.*, fr. 1/6 ; *t.*, fr. 1/– ; *d.*, fr. 2/–.
  Boarding terms : 6/– per day ; 35/– per week.

Lawrence's, (*private*), 52, Pulteney Street.
  Boarding terms : fr. 6/– per day ; fr. 35/– per week.

Edgar (*private*), 2–3, Laura Place : *R.*, single, 2/6 ; double, 4/– ; *b.* or *l.*, 2/– ; *t.*, 6d. ; *d.*, 3/–.
  Boarding terms : fr. 6/– per day ; fr. 42/– per week ; from 10/6 per week-end.

House and Estate Agents.

JOLLY & SON, West of England Property Agents.
Register Free—Telephone, 702.

POWELL & POWELL, 18, Old Bond Street.

FORTT, HATT & BILLINGS, 3, Burton Street.

Bradford-on-Avon.

Castle.

Swan : *R.*, single, 3/– ; double, 6/– ; *b.*, 2/6 ; *l.*, 2/6 ; *t.*, 1/– ; *d.*, 4/– ; *a.*, nil.
  Boarding terms : 10/6 per day ; 63/– per week ; 21/– per week-end. Garage.

New Bear : *R.*, single, 2/6 ; double, 3/6 ; *b.*, 1/6 ; *l.*, 2/6 ; *t.*, fr. 1/3 ; *a.*, 6d. Garage.

Cheddar.

Bath Arms.
Cliff.

Corsham.

Methuen Arms : *R.*, single, fr. 2/– ; double, 3/6 ; *b.*, 2/– ; *l.*, 2/6 ; *t.*, 1/– ; *d.*, 3/6 ; *a.*, 1/–.
  Boarding terms : 63/– per week. Motor Garage.

Royal Oak.
Station.

Glastonbury.

Crown : *R.*, single, fr. 2/– ; double fr. 3/6 ; *b.*, fr. 1/– ; *l.*, fr. 1/9 ; *t.*, 1/– ; *d.*, 2/6 ; *a.*, 6d.
  Boarding terms : 7/6 per day ; 42/– per week ; 15/– per week-end. Garage.

George : *R.*, single, fr. 4/6 ; double, 8/– ; *b.* or *l.*, 2/6 ; *t.*, 1/– ; *d.*, 4/– ; *a.*, 1/6.
  Boarding terms : 10/6 per day ; 63/– per week ; 21/– per week-end. Garage.

Abbey (*temp.*).

Keynsham.

Wingrove.

Lamb and Lark : *R.* and *b.*, fr. 3/– ; *l.*, fr. 1/– ; *t.*, fr. 6d. ; *d.*, fr. 1/6 ; *a.*, nil.
  Boarding terms : fr. 5/6 per day ; fr. 30/– per week ; fr. 8/– per week-end. Garage.

Limpley Stoke.

Hydropathic.

Wells.

Red Lion.

Swan : *R.*, single, 4/6 ; double, 9/– ; *b.*, 2/6 ; *l.*, 3/– ; *t.*, 1/– ; *d.*, 4/6.
  Boarding terms : fr. 10/6 per day ; fr. 63/– per week. Garage.

White Hart.
Star.
Mitre, Sadler Street.

PRELIMINARY INFORMATION.

" Like a Queen enchanted that may not laugh or weep,
  Glad at heart and guarded from change and care like ours,
  Girt about with beauty by days and nights that creep
  Soft as breathless ripples that softly shoreward sweep,
  Lies the lovely city whose grace no grief deflowers.
  Age and grey forgetfulness, time that shifts and veers,
  Touch not thee, our fairest, whose charm no rival nears,
  Hailed as England's Florence by one whose praise gives grace,
  Landor, once thy lover, a name that love reveres,
  Dawn and noon and sunset are one before thy face."
                                        A. C. Swinburne.

IN this section are summarized, in alphabetical order, a number of miscellaneous items of interest and importance to visitors.

Assembly Rooms.

The first Assembly Rooms were erected in 1708 on the site now occupied by the Royal Literary and Scientific Institution. Twelve years later they were enlarged from designs by Killigrew. The Kingston Assembly Rooms, as they were named, were closed in 1820. The architect, Wood senior, built in 1728 the Wiltshire Assembly Rooms, so called after Mrs. Wiltshire and her son, who were, in succession, lessees. It was during the son's time that Beau Nash held sway in Bath, and that the famous Master of Ceremonies lost his reputation owing to the gambling-table scandal.

The present **Assembly Rooms** in Bennet Street were designed by the architect, Wood junior, and, after a building expenditure of £20,000, were opened in October, 1771. Although the exterior is neither beautiful nor very imposing, the interior forms one of the finest and most convenient suites of rooms in the kingdom. For nearly a century and a half the building has contributed to the gaiety of existence in Bath. Its fame is enshrined in the comedies of Sheridan, who was present at the opening and wrote a poem on the occasion;

and Jane Austen and Dickens have immortalized it in their works. The present proprietors, while preserving the best traditions of the past, have adorned the place in keeping with modern taste and requirements.

Electric light is installed throughout, and brilliant effects of illumination are obtained by the aid of the cut-glass Vauxhall candelabra.

The high standard maintained by the Assembly Rooms for generations as a place of entertainment is being continued, and all the most famous vocalists and lecturers have at some time appeared here. Concerts and dramatic entertainments, popular assemblies and dances, are arranged here as of old ; and there are also the usual Society functions and Subscription Balls at Christmas, Easter and other times.

Banks.

Capital and Counties, 47, Milsom Street ; *Lloyds*, Milsom Street, and 1, George Street ; *London City and Midland*, 45, Milsom Street ; *National Provincial*, York Buildings, corner of Milsom Street ; *Parr's*, 39, Milsom Street ; *Union of London and Smith's*, High Street.

Boating.

There is good boating on the Avon between Bathwick and Bathampton ; also at Saltford, about 5 miles below the city. An annual regatta is conducted under the joint auspices of the rowing clubs of Bath and Bristol.

The river at Bath is highly picturesque. The reach of water to Bathampton, and over the weirs to Warley, passes through one of the most charming bits of the Avon Valley.

The Bath Boating Company own two boating stations, at which boats and canoes can be hired by the month, week, day or hour. The Company have also a boathouse at Saltford.

The **Avon Rowing Club** has its headquarters at the Bath Boating Company's Station, Bathwick, where there is a commodious club-room. The Club also possesses a boathouse at Saltford. Visitors introduced by members, 10s. 6d. first month, and 5s. per month afterwards. Members have the privilege of cheap return tickets by railway to Saltford and Kelston.

Bowls.

Great expense and care have been expended in bringing to perfection the greens of the **Bath Bowling Club.** They are situated in a delightful spot in a corner of the Recreation Ground. Visitors are admitted to temporary membership on application to the Secretary, 41, Milsom Street. There is also a public green in Alexandra Park.

Climate and Situation.

The situation of the city, nestling amid hills, is singularly beautiful. The hills, from which fine views may be gained of Bath and the picturesque country beyond, form a protection from the prevailing winds, which are from the west ; and the consequent mild winter climate makes the place a favourite resort for invalids during the cold months. The growth of the city has caused long lines of beautiful residential streets to be laid up the slopes of the hills ; and on those loftier sites, such as Lansdown (750 feet above sea-level) and Combe Down (550 feet), the air is very bracing.

Bath is noted for possessing a great variety of climates within a comparatively circumscribed area. Central Bath has an equable climate, genial in the coldest weather and eminently suitable for invalids and elderly people ; while modern developments of electric tramcars, motor omnibuses and taxicabs, have brought within easy reach the heights of Lansdown on the north and those of Combe Down on the south.

The river Avon, coming northward from Limpley Stoke, enters the Bath valley at Bathford, and is deflected sharply to the south-west. Making another curve round the spur of Lansdown, it flows from Bath in a north-westerly direction. The course of the river through the City, being like the letter S, shows the variety of aspects of the slopes bordering the river, and, with the different subsoils, explains the differences of temperature found in a limited space.

The following records relate to Central Bath, a low-lying area of about 600 acres :—

Rainfall.—Observations taken at the Royal Literary and Scientific Institution, extending over forty years, give the mean annual rainfall as 30·48 inches.

Temperature.—Observations taken at the Central Climatic Station, Henrietta Park, for ten years give a mean temperature of 49·5° F. The mean winter temperature is 41°, spring 52°, summer 59°, autumn 46°. February is the coldest month, the average mean temperature being 39°, and July the hottest, with an average of 61·5°.

Sunshine.—Bath is well placed for getting a full amount of winter sunshine ; compared with the north-east of England it has 51 hours more " possible sunshine " in the winter, and 58 hours less " possible sunshine " in the summer. The records for ten years show an average of 243 hours " bright sunshine " during the winter months, 557 hours during the spring, 576 hours during the summer and 199 during the autumn months ; a yearly average of 1,575 hours of bright sunshine.

Clubs.

The **Bath and County Club,** 21 and 22, Queen Square, is open to strangers, resident for a short period, who are introduced by permanent members.

The **Constitutional Club,** Edgar Buildings, is designed to promote the objects of the Unionist party. Visitors, duly introduced, are admitted as temporary members at a monthly fee of 5s.

The **Bath and County Ladies' Club** is in Milsom Street. Visitors, on being proposed and seconded by two members, may be admitted to temporary membership at a subscription of 2s. weekly, or 5s. monthly.

Churches and Chapels,
with hours of Sunday services :—

The Abbey, St. Peter and St. Paul—11, 4 and 7.
Christ, top of Russell Street—11, 3 and 6.30.
St. Andrew's, Julian Road—11, 3 and 6.30.
St. James's, Stall Street—11 and 6.30.
St. John's, Bathwick, near Cleveland Bridge—10.30, 3.30 and 7.
St. John's, near Gas Works—11 and 6.30.
St. Luke's, near Devonshire Buildings—11 and 6.30.
St. Mark's, Lyncombe—11 and 6.30.
St. Mary's, Bathwick (Raby Place)—11, 3.15 and 6.30.
St. Matthew's, Widcombe—11 and 6.30.
St. Michael's, Broad Street—11 and 6.30.
St. Paul's, Queen Square—11 and 6.30.
St. Saviour's, Larkhall—11 and 6.30.
St. Stephen's, Lansdown Road—11 and 6.30.
St. Swithin's, Walcot—11 and 6.30.

St. Peter's, East Twerton—11 and 6.30.

Trinity, James Street, near Midland Station—11, 3 and 6.30.

Widcombe Old Church (Widcombe Crescent)—11 and 3.

Roman Catholic, St. John's, South Parade—11, 3, and 6.30.

Roman Catholic, St. Mary's, Julian Road—11, 3.30 and 6.30.

Catholic Apostolic, Vineyards—10, 5 and 6.

Moravian Episcopal, Charlotte Street—11 and 6.30.

EPISCOPAL CHAPELS.

All Saints', Lansdown Crescent—11, 3.15 and 6.30.

Kensington, Kensington Place—11 and 6.30.

Mineral Water Hospital—11 and 3.

Mission Chapel, Corn Street—6.30.

Portland, Harley Street, Julian Road—11 and 6.30.

St. Michael's, Hetling Court—11 and 3.

St. Mary Magdalen, Holloway—11 and 3.

Thomas Street—11 and 6.30.

NONCONFORMIST.

Baptist, Ebenezer (Canal Bridge), Manvers Street and Hay Hill—11 and 6.30.

   ,,   Bethesda, Weymouth Street, Walcot—3 and 6.30.

Congregational, Argyle Street and Charlotte Street—11 and 6.30.

Disciples of Christ, Chandos Hall, Westgate Buildings—11 and 6.30.

Friends', York Street—11 and 6.30.

Countess of Huntingdon's, Vineyards—11 and 6.30.

New Church, Henry Street—11 and 6.30.

Presbyterian, Brock Street—11 and 6.30.

Primitive Methodist, Westgate Buildings and Claremont—11 and 6.30.

Unitarian, Trim Street—11 and 6.30.

Wesleyan, New King Street and Walcot—11 and 6.30.

Cricket.

The **Lansdown Cricket Club** is famous as well for its pitches as for its position in the cricket world. Visitors are admitted to membership at a reduced fee. There is, in the centre of the city, a fine Recreation Ground, where first-class County Championship matches are played.

Croquet

is played on the Recreation Ground. Particulars, with terms of temporary membership for visitors, may be had on application to the Secretary, Bath and County Recreation Ground Company, Limited, 41, Milsom Street.

DISTANCES—FISHING—GEOLOGY

Distances from Bath.

	MILES.			MILES.
Birmingham . . .	103	London		107
Bradford (Yorks). .	217	Manchester . . .		188
Bridgwater . . .	45	Newcastle-on-Tyne .		304
Bristol	12	Nottingham . . .		151
Cheltenham . . .	56	Oxford		64
Derby	135	Plymouth		140
Exeter	87	Sheffield		161
Frome	13½	Shrewsbury . . .		174
Gloucester . . .	49	Swindon		37
Leeds	203	Taunton		57
Liverpool	201	Trowbridge . . .		11

Early Closing.

The Early Closing Day is Thursday.

Fishing.

There is good fishing in the **Avon** and in the **Kennet and Avon Canal**, the principal sport being with pike, roach, perch and gudgeon. Trout of fair size are also to be had. Some of the best swims are in the possession of the **Bath Angling Association**. Day tickets, 1s., and weekly tickets, 2s. 6d., can be obtained of Mr. R. Chambers, Fishing Tackle Manufacturer, 40, Walcot Street.

Geology.

The roads are dry on the surrounding slopes, being bedded in the cap of Great Oolite, or Bath Stone, which is here superficial and from 100 to 200 feet in thickness. Underlying this is the Fullers' Earth formation, more easily denuded, and giving the gradual slopes up to the higher levels. Immediately under the Fullers' Earth is the Inferior Oolite, the outcrop of which may be seen in the lane leading down to the picturesque village of Charlcombe. The Midford Sands (Upper Lias) come next in order, the formation being easily recognized by the alternation of level ground and sudden slopes. Beneath the Midford Sands are the Lias Clay and Rock on which central Bath is built ; but considerable deposits of Mammal drift gravel lie in the bend of the river. The subsoil of Henrietta or Bathwick Park is Gravel, and here the Central Climatic Station is placed ; a second station is on the Fullers' Earth at Kingswood School ; a third on the Oolite of Claverton Down, and a fourth on the Lias at Combe Park.

BATH, FROM BEECHEN CLIFF.

BATH ABBEY AND INSTITUTION GARDENS.

GOLF—HOCKEY

The mean elevation of the city of Bath is 285 feet above sea-level, or 225 feet above London.

Combe Down is 550 feet above sea-level, or 200 feet lower than Lansdown; but, the strata being inclined in that direction, it, too, is capped by the Great Oolite. It was by observing the similarity of the outcropping rocks of the Bath Valley that William Smith, the Father of English Geology, in 1795 realized the continuity of various strata and enunciated the first principles of modern geology.

Golf.

The course of the **Bath Golf Club** (18 holes), on Hampton Down, commands fine views over the Avon Valley. Visitors (introduced by a member), 2/- day; 7/6 week; 20/- month.

The **Bath Ladies' Golf Club** has a strong membership, and, like the other clubs, welcomes visitors as temporary members (1/6 day; 5/- week; 15/- month).

The links of the **Lansdown Golf Club** (18 holes) are 3½ miles from the Guildhall; but arrangements are made with the York House and Lansdown Mews to take players up and bring them back at specially low terms. In addition, a motor 'bus service, belonging to the Electric Trams Co., runs up Lansdown. A grand and varied view, extending into seven counties and across the Bristol Channel to the Welsh hills, is to be obtained from the twelfth green on a clear day; while from the seventh green the Malvern Hills are visible. The fourth green is on Derby Point, 760 feet above sea-level, the highest part of Lansdown. The annual subscription is £2 2s., with a £1 1s. entrance fee. Ladies, £1 1s., no entrance fee. Family tickets are issued at £4 4s., with an entrance fee of one guinea. Visitors may be introduced by a member at a daily fee of 2s. Daily green fees, Sundays, 2s. 6d.; other days: men, 2s.; ladies, 1s. 6d.

At the opposite side of the valley, on Odd Down, close to the tramway route, is the **Bladud Golf Club** with a very sporting 9-hole course, 500 feet above sea-level. Green fees 1/- day, (Saturdays 2/-), 5/- week, 10/6 month.

Hockey

is played on the Recreation Ground; particulars, with terms of temporary membership for visitors, may be had from the Secretary of the Bath and County Recreation Ground Company, Limited, 41, Milsom Street.

Hunting.

The **Duke of Beaufort's Hunt** and other packs meet within easy distance of Bath. The **Bath & County Harriers** have their headquarters at Claverton Down, within two miles of the city. Hunting can be had six days a week.

Local Government.

Bath is a County Borough, and has a Corporation consisting of a Mayor, fourteen Aldermen and forty-two Councillors. The city is divided into seven wards.

Bath returns two members to Parliament, and includes a portion of the parish of Twerton in its parliamentary division.

Markets.

Wednesday and Saturday are the market days. The Market is in High Street. The Cattle Market is held on Wednesdays, the Corn Market on Thursdays.

Masonic Lodges.

Royal Cumberland, No. 41 ; **Honor Lodge**, No. 376 ; **Chapter Royal Sussex**, No. 51 ; **Chapter Royal Albert Edward**, No. 906. The Masonic Hall is in Manvers Place.

Municipal Buildings.

These are situated at the corner of High Street, on the north side of the Abbey. The **Guildhall**, which forms the front centre of the block, is the oldest part of the buildings, the foundation stone having been laid in 1776. It is in the Georgian style. The **Banqueting Hall**, or Ball Room, a stately chamber, contains several portraits of local and national interest. Here are pictured the Earl of Chatham, who, as Mr. Pitt, represented Bath in Parliament ; other Members, such as Earl Camden and Marshal Wade ; Ralph Allen, who welcomed at his mansion of Prior Park the leading figures in English religious and literary life ; Alderman Hunt, five times Mayor of Bath ; Beau Nash, once the leader, and Anstey, the satirist of the local world of fashion. Here also figure George III and his Consort, and Frederick, Prince of Wales, father of George III. This prince was one whom Bath delighted to honour ; and he showed his gratitude by presenting to the Corporation a splendid silver cup, which is still on State occasions passed round in honour of the loyal toast.

The **New Municipal Buildings,** an addition to the civic structure, were opened in 1894. In 1900 the block was completed by the erection of the **Victoria Art Gallery.** There are now under one roof, Council Chamber and Banqueting Hall, Corporation offices, Police Courts and Fire Brigade stations, Technical Schools, Reference Library, and Art Gallery.

Museums and Art Galleries.

The **Holburne Art Museum,** so called because its treasures were given to the city by the late Mary Anne Barbara Holburne, includes a variety of antiquities, valuable paintings and a collection of gold and silver plate and china. It has recently been transferred to new quarters at the end of Pulteney Street. The Museum is open free daily from 11 to 4.

There is also an interesting Museum in the buildings of the **Royal Literary and Scientific Association**.

The **Victoria Art Gallery,** opened in 1900 as a memorial of Queen Victoria's Diamond Jubilee, is situated in the Municipal Buildings.

In **the Grand Pump Room** and adjoining **Museum** may be seen the valuable collection of Roman antiquities unearthed in the vicinity of the Baths.

Railway Stations.

The **Great Western Station** is in Railway Place, in the south of the city. Central Bath may be reached by way of Manvers Street (opposite the Station) and Pierrepont Street, which leads into the North Parade ; or by way of Dorchester Street **and** along Southgate Street into Stall Street.

The **Midland Railway Station,** which also serves the **Somerset and Dorset Line,** is at the corner of James Street and Seymour Street, directly west of central Bath.

Royal Literary and Scientific Institution.

Open daily (except Sundays) from 9 a.m. to 10 p.m.

This building, in the ancient thoroughfare known as Terrace Walks, faces the east end of York Street, and stands on the site of the old Assembly Rooms destroyed by fire in 1820. The Institution, established in 1824, contains reading room, chess room, smoking room, a library for the use of members, a museum and a lecture hall.

The **Library,** of over 20,000 volumes, includes many valuable works of reference and rare volumes. Of special interest is a collection of books on science and natural history known as the *Jenyns Library,* bequeathed by the Rev. Leonard Blomefield, a local naturalist There is also a good circulating

ROYAL LITERARY INSTITUTION

library for the use of members, and the leading newspapers and magazines are taken.

The **Museum** (*open free on Thursdays ; on other days 2d.*). In the vestibules and lobbies are many of the Roman antiquities found in and around Bath. The geological collection made by Mr. Charles Moore, and purchased by subscription in 1878, is placed in one of the upper rooms. It is of extreme interest in relation to the Rhætic beds, which Mr. Moore studied with patient industry and learned insight for many years. The Saurian specimens from the Lower Lias, and the fish and reptiles from the Upper Lias, will also appeal to the student of geology.

In an adjoining gallery is a valuable mineralogical collection made by Mr. Frederick Field, and in another gallery is the historical and anthropological museum. Also exhibited here are the Godfrey ornithological collection and the Duncan Museum of local natural history.

The lecture room is a large and well-lighted apartment. On the ceiling are four paintings by Cassali that were formerly among the decorations of Fonthill Abbey.

Temporary residents in Bath are admitted to membership at half the usual rates, particulars of which may be had on application at the Institution.

Tennis.

The **Combe Park Lawn Tennis Club** was founded in 1895. Temporary membership is allowed to visitors for a small payment on the introduction of a member.

Lansdown Tennis Club, Lansdown Road ; **Oldfield Lawn Tennis Club,** Bloomfield Gardens.

Tennis is also played on the Recreation Ground ; terms on application to the Secretary, Bath and County Recreation Ground Company, Limited, 41, Milsom Street.

Theatres, etc.

The **Theatre Royal,** in Saw Close, rebuilt in 1862-3 after a fire, accommodates 1,600 persons, and is a well-constructed and attractive building. The centenary of the opening of the first Bath Theatre Royal was celebrated on October 13, 1905. Bath obtained the first Theatre Royal in the Provinces, the patent being granted in 1768. Only about four patent theatres now remain, of which Bath is one.

The **Palace Theatre of Varieties** is also in Saw Close.

There are several well-appointed **Picture Palaces.**

HISTORIC BATH.

THE virtues of the fair city of Bath have stood the stern
test of time. For nearly two thousand years—probably longer—its healing waters have attracted a succession
of pilgrims anxious to find, amid pleasant country and interesting social surroundings, a cure for the ills of the flesh.

It is the custom to begin the story of Bath with the myth
of King Bladud, and to continue it with the occupation of
the Romans; but to read aright the annals of this most
ancient city we must start at a period compared with which
the doings of Bladud and the coming of the Romans were
comparatively modern events.

South of Bath, behind the Great Western Railway Station,
is **Beechen Cliff,** rising by a steep ascent to a height of 400
feet. It may be reached in a few minutes by the bridge at
the bottom of Southgate Street, and the view of Bath from
the summit will repay the climb. Immediately below is the
Avon, and beyond towers and spires, squares and parks,
crescents and public buildings, are pictured as in a coloured
map. If the visitor will look upon the surrounding hills which
form " the nest-like hollow where the City of Bath reposes,"
and particularly upon the more distant height towards the
north-east, he will see the spot which links Bath with times
so far anterior to the Roman period as to verge upon the
pre-historic. The height in the north-east, beyond Bath, is
known as—

Solsbury Hill.

It belongs to the southern extremity of the Cotswolds,
and yet is an almost isolated eminence, so situated that it
commands a more extended view of the Avon Valley than is
gained from any of the neighbouring hills. Its flat top, of
about half the diameter of its base, has to be carefully con-

sidered in relation to the ancient puzzle that we, with the assistance of the historian Earle, are trying to unravel.

In the *Itinerary of Antoninus*, Bath is mentioned under the name of *Aquæ Solis*, i.e. the Waters of the Sun ; and were it not for the historical existence of Solsbury, it would have been a fair conclusion that the name was derived from the Latin *sol*. " It seems clear from the inscribed stones that have been from time to time dug out in various parts of Bath, that under this name Solis we have something more interesting to us than the genitive case of *sol*, the sun. It is found spelt Sul in the connection *deæ Sul-Minervæ*, which shows that it was the name of a divinity, and that this Sul was identified in attributions with the Roman Minerva. Meanwhile, we take the fact as established that Solis—however understood or misunderstood by the Romans—represents Sul, a local and native sacred name which these waters owned before ever a Roman bathed in them."

The Ancient Fortress of Bath.

It is a matter of elementary knowledge that the termination " bury " means a fort or stronghold ; and the conclusion cannot be doubted that the height of Solsbury was a natural fortress on which depended the protection of some neighbouring population. A position of such natural strength in an age when the country was split into dozens of petty kingships, each constantly warring against the others, would naturally attract a population craving for safety. Many a town, such as Edinburgh and Durham, can trace its origin to the protecting attraction of some mediæval castle. So in ages more remote, when an isolated hill was the best refuge, these hills became in like manner the parents of cities.

Solsbury Hill is not of great height, but its slopes are steep enough for defence, and the area of 30 acres at the top would accommodate thousands. From their dwellings by the riverside the people would hasten to the protecting hill when danger threatened, and there remain until the trouble was for the time over ; while their water would be supplied by the springs flowing out of crevices in the slopes.

It matters little whether it actually gave a population to the city beneath it, or only fostered the growth of the city by its facilities for retreat. In any case, Solsbury marks the dawn of the history of Bath. It is historic truth that the word Solis in the *Aquæ Solis*, inscribed on so many Roman stones to be seen in Bath, represents not a Roman but a native divinity, honoured in the land for ages before the coming of the legions from Italy.

The Two Myths of Bath.

It has been well said that a mythical origin crowns the history of a place with an aristocratic character. A myth is not an invention for the sake of fraud; it is a story which somehow, no one knows how, came to occupy the place of history in the popular belief. As Gog and Magog are to London, and Romulus and Remus to Rome, so is the myth of Bladud to Bath—a halo of romance gleaming over the trackless waste of an unknown past.

The Early Myth

is recorded solemnly as actual history in the pages of Geoffry of Monmouth; and it has more than a local interest in its allusion to King Lear and his daughters. The following is a translation of Geoffry's history :—

"Bladud, son and successor of the British King Hudibras, was a master of the black art, and the devil told him whatever he wanted to know. This famous King Bladud made the Bath through magic skill. A cunning stone as big as a tree was laid in the welling spring, and that made the water hot and healed the sick people. Hard by the Bath he made a temple in honour of a heathen goddess; and if you want to know her name it was Minerva. In this temple a continual fire was kept up in honour of Minerva, and Bladud's fame was spread abroad. But he was for ever devising some new wonder, and by and by he gave out that he was about to fly in the air like a bird.

"So he had wings made to his own destruction. He fitted on his pinions and mounted in the air with a strong and bold flight. But lo! he fell in with contrary winds, and his strength failed; the strings snapped, his rigging got out of order, and down he fell. He pitched on the roof of Apollo's temple, and was dashed to pieces.

"Bladud had reigned twenty years, and he left behind him a son called Lear, who reigned after him—a long reign —for sixty years. This King Lear had no son, but three daughters, Goneril, Regan and Cordelia."

Every myth with any claim to respectability must at one time have been accepted as veracious history, and the later story of Bladud, even so comparatively recently as the sixteenth century, was regarded as uncoloured fact. It is handed down by Warner, a Bath historian, who, of course, regarded it as a myth.

Bladud and the Swine.

" About five-and-thirty centuries ago Lud Hudibras swayed the sceptre of Britain. Bladud was the heir apparent of this monarch, a prince of the highest expectations, the darling of his parents, and the delight of the court. This amiable personage became a leper, and the courtiers prevailed upon his reluctant father to banish him, lest he should contaminate their immaculate circle with this horrible malady.

" Lud Hudibras, therefore, dismissed the Prince with tears and blessings ; to which the Queen added a brilliant ring as a mark by which he might make himself known should he get rid of his disease. Shut out from society, Bladud could now only aspire to the meanest employments ; and having travelled as far as Keynsham, a village about six miles from Bath, he offered himself to a man of that village, who dealt largely in pigs, to take charge of these respectable animals.

" Bladud soon discovered that he had communicated his disorder to the herd ; and, dreading the displeasure of his patron, he requested that he might drive his charge to the opposite side of the river, under the pretext that the acorns were finer there. The owner complied with his request ; and Bladud, passing the river at a shallow since called Swineford, conducted his pigs to the hills which hung over the northern side of Bath. The health-dispensing springs of this place stole at that time disregarded through the valley.

" The swine, however, led by instinct, soon discovered the treasure, and, anxious to rid themselves of the disease, quitted their keeper, rushed violently down the hill, and plunged into the muddy morass below. The royal swineherd, having seduced them away by the sight of a bag of acorns, led them back to their pens. No sooner, however, had he washed from them the mud than he perceived that the animals had already shed the scabby marks of their disorder.

" Bladud wisely concluded that there could be no effect without an adequate cause. If the waters cured the hogs of the leprosy, they would be equally beneficial to a man. He proceeded to bathe himself in them, and had the inexpressible happiness to find himself cleansed from his disease."

A Prehistoric Aviator.

" Bladud," continues Warner, " marched back the pigs to his patron, returned to Court, was acknowledged with rapture, proceeded to the place where he had found his cure,

PULTENEY STREET.

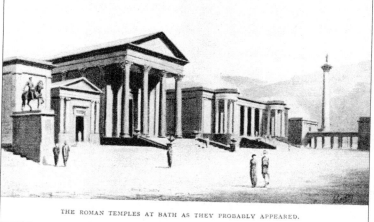

THE ROMAN TEMPLES AT BATH AS THEY PROBABLY APPEARED.

cleaned the springs, erected baths, and built a splendid city on the spot. Here he lived and reigned for many years with great honour; but getting foolish as he became old, and scorning any longer to tread the earth like a common mortal, he determined to tread the air on a pair of wings which he had constructed. On a certain day he sprang from the pinnacle of a temple which he had founded to Minerva, at Bath, tumbled instantly to the ground, and at once put an end to his life."

" Deficient as the above account is," continues Warner, " in anything that could stamp it with probability, the inhabitants of Bath both gave credit to, and valued themselves upon, the British origin of their city; and the belief in Bladud formed part of the creed of every true Bath man."

There is preserved in the British Museum, in the form of a written footnote to the above account, the following curious record of credulity with regard to the Bladud story : " We whose names are hereunder written, natives of the city of Bath, having perused the above tradition, do think it very truly and faithfully related—as witness our hands this first day of November, 1741."

Early British Occupation.

The most sceptical will admit that whether Bladud, " eighth in succession from Brute, the great-grandson of Æneas," and consequently the great-great-grandson of no less a personage than Venus, did or did not feed swine on the site of the present Pump Room, there is still every possibility that the virtues of the Bath waters were known to the Britons. The hill-girdled country on which Bath stands was at the time of the Roman invasion the seat of an important British fortress, whose occupants must have known the healing efficacy of the springs. The Romans evidently lost no time in testing their quality.

Roman Remains in Bath.

There is no town in England so rich in Roman remains as Bath. From 44 to 410 A.D. the Romans held sway in Britain, and it was probably at an early period of their occupation that they appreciated the virtues of the hot springs and founded the city.

The remains of their baths add another to those monuments of constructive labour which this nation of architectural

Titans have left behind them in every quarter of their Empire. Here, as elsewhere, they seem to have planned as for a dominion that was to last for ever.

It needs but a glance at these remains to make us sure that the story of Bladud is not entirely fiction. The father of King Lear may not have built the temple to Minerva ; but that such a British temple existed there can be no question, for the symbols of the helmet and owl appear on many a sculptured stone ; and to Minerva these emblems alone belonged.

It is comparatively recently that these Roman remains have been unearthed ; and, extensive though they are, the excavations cover but a very small part of the original site. Could the foundations of the present city be examined, there would certainly be brought to light Roman work compared with which the remains we can look upon are insignificant in size. The ancient baths must, from a calculation based on the parts excavated, have covered an area of 7 acres ; and there would be the lounges and pleasure grounds in addition to the palaces and villas of the Roman residents. The old print reproduced on another page, from the late Mr. J. F. Meehan's collection, probably gives an accurate idea of the appearance of the stately temples.

Recent Excavations.

It was in 1754 that the first discovery of a Roman bath was made, and a century passed before the excavations were continued. The most important work in this direction was begun in 1882 by Major Davis, then City Architect, who, with the zealous co-operation of Councillor J. W. Morris, caused to be unearthed, beneath shops and dwelling-houses, the rectangular bath with a water area of 82 feet by 40 feet. It was coated with lead, obtained probably from the Roman mines in the Mendip Hills.

There have also been discovered the heating chambers of a hot dry bath, or " hypocaust," corresponding in some measure to the system now known as the Turkish. The vestibule of the Roman baths belonged to the present site of the Grand Pump Room ; and its grandeur will be understood by the elaborate and massive sculpture shown on the fragments that have been unearthed.

That the Romans recognized the value of the springs as mineral waters is shown by an excavation, 27 feet beneath the Pump Room, disclosing a flight of stone steps leading to a trough into which pure mineral waters flowed for drinking purposes. Close by were found a drinking cup and two metal flagons, and a bronze tablet with an inscription showing that a Roman lady was cured by drinking from the springs.

The value of the cold douche was also known to them, as is proved by the discovery of the delivery end of a lead pipe which was "laid on" in the early second century from a cold spring that rose on the Lansdown heights.

Aquæ Solis.

The *Sul* of the British period was, as we have already stated, identified by the Romans with their own *Sol* ; and, as Minerva had among her attributes that of stirring men to active life, the wakening cock and the trumpet sounding the *reveillé* were sacred to her ; and she was, among other things, the goddess of medicine. These were evidently the reasons that led the Romans to link their own Minerva with the British *Sul* as co-patronesses of the valley through which the healing waters flowed.

Roman and Provincial Deities.

In Dollinger's *Jew and Gentile* this identification of other gods with their own by the Romans is clearly explained :—

"After the Roman religion had adapted itself to the Grecian, and people in Rome as well as in Greece believed in the identity of gods in both, it appeared to the Romans that the deities of other peoples whom they had subdued showed a strong affinity to their own ; only the names, they thought, were different ; in principle and essence they were the same forms in different localities.

"The natives of the different countries were on their side quite content that their gods, those of the vanquished and the subject, should turn out identical with those of their victors and rulers. Accordingly, temples were speedily raised in the provinces, in which Roman and barbarous deities exchanged names and attributes with one another, little claim as they had to personify the same thought originally."

Sul and Minerva.

An example of the linking of the British and Roman deities may be seen on an altar discovered in 1774 near to the Hot Spring Bath. The L.M. at the close of the following inscription stands for *libens merito*, which, as is shown in similar records, is an abbreviation of *votum solvit libens merito*, i.e., " the votary fulfils cheerfully the vow which he acknowledges as due for mercies rendered : "—

D E A E

S V L I   M I

N E R V A E

S V L I N V S

M A T V

R I   F I L

I V S   L.M.

Two Roman Roads

passed through the city—the **Fosse** and the **Via Julia**—and it was along these roads, and not in their temples, that the Romans placed their sepulchral monuments, so that the passer-by might see them with their sculptured appeal, *Siste Viator* (Pause, O Traveller !), and grow thoughtful over the symbols of mortality. The **Forum** was situated in the space now existing between the Abbey Church and the Pump Room Hotel.

The Earliest Roman Baths

are supposed to have been founded either by Vespasian or during the reign of his son Titus. " These baths," says a recent writer, " must have witnessed a thousand diversified scenes, as they were the great places of resort of the Roman people. The poet here recited his last composition, and the athletes excited the luxurious bather with a thousand feats of strength ; the song and the loud laugh caught the ear of many an old warrior as he anointed himself luxuriously with the precious ointments then in use ; and little did the busy crowd beneath its portico imagine that a few centuries would bury it deep in the earth, and that the conqueror who was to come after them would inter the dead over the very spot that once contributed to the vigour of the living."

The Britons in Bath.

About the year 410 the Romans withdrew from Britain for the defence of their capital against the northern invaders. Of the interval between the departure of the Romans and the coming of the Anglo-Saxons little is known. As a usually clear historian of Bath has said, in a Johnsonian phrase, the period can be best described as " a distant, inarticulate reverberation of internal convulsion." Sul-Minerva was no longer an object of reverence, for the British had accepted Christianity, and the heathen temple was allowed to fall into ruin. *Solis* dropped out of the city's name, which was now *Aquæ* alone. " This," writes Earle, " in British pronunciation and orthography took the form *Ake*, with which was presently coupled the syllable *man*, which was the British word for place. *Akeman* was a British compound embodying a Roman element, and it signified the place known by the name of Aquæ. The Roman road from London, which passed through Oxfordshire, and by Marlborough to Akeman (Bath) was called Akeman Street."

The Saxons in Bath.

Step by step the Anglo-Saxons drove the British westward ; and in course of time the name of the city was enlarged by them from Akeman to *Akemanceaster*. But with the discovery of the virtues of the hot springs seems to have come a dislike to the tongue-twisting name of their own invention, and Akemanceaster was subsequently changed for Hoete Bathum—the Hot Baths.

The Saxons gave to the city a new name, but robbed it of its splendour. When Ceawlin of Wessex took it by storm in 577 he made a ruin of palaces, baths and temples, and for years the once fair city lay a desolate heap. " Its hot waters were allowed to flood its courts and corridors until the washings of the land on which the baths had been excavated gradually covered the remains of their magnificence, and thus preserved them for thirteen centuries as a witness to the grandeur of the Roman idea."

The discovery of the medicinal qualities of the hot springs, and the foundation of a religious house in 676 by the Saxon king Osric, caused a revival of the city's fame, but the old glory of Bath was not yet renewed.

Bath Abbey in Olden Times.

Nearly the whole of the Saxon documents concerning Bath are connected with the history of its Abbey Church ; and the growing importance of the Minster is proved by its choice as the scene of the crowning of King Edgar. The citizens made much of King Edgar at his crowning, and in return he showed special favour to their city.

JOHN DE VILLULA

Even in comparatively modern times the coronation festivities had an echo; for Leland, writing in the sixteenth century, speaks of the gratitude of the men of Bath for the goodness shown to their city in ancient times by King Edgar, "They pray," he says, "in all the ceremonies for his soule; and at Whitsunday tide, at the which time men say that Eadgar ther was crownid, ther is a king elected at Bath every yere of the townesmen in the joyful remembrance of King Eadgar, and the privileges gyven to the town by him. This king is fested, and his adherents, by the richest man of the town."

In the eighteenth century, when society bowed low before Beau Nash, "King of Bath," the custom dating from Edgar's reign was pleaded as an excuse for modern folly.

The period of over seven centuries between the reigns of King Edgar and "King Nash" was a depressing one in the history of Bath. When Rufus became King there was an unsuccessful rising in favour of his elder brother, Robert, and in the struggle that took place in the West, Bath was sacked and burnt. For three years (1087 to 1090) it remained a desolation. Then—

John de Villula,

an honoured name in the history of Bath, came to the rescue. He was a native of Tours, and was both physician and chaplain to William II, who, seeming to have a liking for this doctor of bodies and souls, sold him the bishopric of Wells. But Bath was more attractive to him as a residence, and he chose that city as his episcopal seat, becoming the first Bishop of Bath and Wells.

The Bishop was as eager for a bargain as the King was for money; and Bath being a royal possession, Villula offered for it the sum of 500 marks. Rufus accepted, and threw in as makeweight the Abbey, the Mint, and the Baths. The city flourished under the rule of this king-bishop, for not only did he rebuild the Abbey, but "restored the citizens' houses that had been burnt or ruined, and became a refounder of Bath, raising a new city out of the ashes of the old."

For nearly a century the bishops of the diocese were sovereign lords of Bath, possessing in almost every particular the powers of a king over local property and affairs. The last of these king-bishops was the foreigner Savaric, who, by arrangement with Richard Cœur de Lion, exchanged Bath for Glastonbury, and to his death styled himself Bishop of Glastonbury. Thus did Bath pass again into the keeping of the Crown, and once more fell into decay.

Queen Elizabeth at Bath.

In the year 1590 a new Charter was given by Queen Elizabeth, enlarging the powers and area of the Corporation. The hot springs had again become popular, and better local government was an urgent need. In the following year Elizabeth paid a visit to her godson, Sir John Harington, at Kelston, and was one day driven into Bath. But she carried away an unpleasant impression of the poor paving and foul smells from open sewers. Sir John Harington, in a letter addressed to Lord Burleigh, wrote as follows :—

" The citie of Bathe, my Lord, being both poore enough and proude enough, hath, since her Highnesse being there, wonderfully beautified itselfe in fine houses for vitualling and lodging, but decayes fast. . . .

" The fair church her Highnesse gave order should be re-edified, stands at a stay ; and their common sewer, which before stood in an ill-place, stands now in no place, for they have not any at all ; which for a towne so plentifullye served of water, in a countrey so well provided of stone, in a place resorted unto so greatly, methinke seemeth an unworthie and dishonourable thing." Then Sir John went on to say that if the funds were honestly applied, " I would not doubt of a ruinate church to make a reverent church, and of an unsavorie town a most sweet town."

This letter was written about 1591, yet forty years later a competent authority had thus to speak of Bath :—

" The streets are dung-hills, slaughterhouses ʃand pig-sties ; the butchers dress their meat at their own doors, while pigs wallow in the mire. The baths are bear-gardens, where passers-by pelt the bathers with dead cats and dogs."

Another Royal Visit to Bath.

Thirteen years later the Queen of Charles I visited the city, and again royal favour increased its popularity among visitors, so that the Corporation fussily drew up laws for better government—with what success may be gathered from a description of the place as it appeared about sixty years afterwards :—

" Bath was under the dominion of a gang of well-dressed roughs, gamesters and adventurers. Swords and bludgeons were flourished upon the promenades. Ladies in the streets, and even in the baths, were greeted with offensive gibe. The evening entertainments were nightly invaded by drunken ruffians, swaggering about with swords or riding whips, lolling on settees with mud-bespattered boots."

Bath in the Seventeenth Century.

Macaulay, in Chapter III of his *History of England*, thus describes, from information given in *Evelyn's Diary* (1654) and *Pepys' Diary* (1668), and from the works of local writers, the condition of Bath in the seventeenth century :

" At the head of English watering-places, without a rival, was Bath. The springs of that city had been renowned from the times of the Romans. It had been, during many centuries, the seat of a Bishop. The sick repaired thither from every part of the realm. The King sometimes held his court there. Nevertheless, Bath was then a maze of only four or five hundred houses, crowded within an old wall in the vicinity of the Avon. . . . Travellers complained loudly of the narrowness and meanness of its streets. That beautiful city which charms even eyes familiar with the masterpieces of Bramante and Palladio, and which the genius of Anstey and of Smollet, of Frances Burney and of Jane Austen, has made classic ground, had not begun to exist. Milsom Street itself was an open field lying far beyond the walls ; and hedgerows intersected the space which is now covered by the Crescent and the Circus. . . . A writer who published an account of that city about sixty years after the Revolution assures us that, in his younger days, the gentlemen who visited the springs slept in rooms hardly as good as garrets. The floors of the dining-rooms were uncarpeted, and were coloured brown with a wash made of soot and small beer in order to hide the dirt. . . . The best apartments were hung with coarse woollen stuff, and were furnished with rush-bottomed chairs."

Very interesting is the story of how Bath quickly rose from the condition of a neglected provincial town into, as Mr. Traill related in an interesting article on *Two Centuries of Bath*, " a sort of second capital of English fashion, the headquarters for certain seasons of the year of all that was gay and witty and wicked and fascinating and frivolous in English society."

THE ASSEMBLY ROOMS (18TH CENTURY).

(From a rare print in the collection of the late Mr. J. F. Meehan, Bath.)

THE COMFORTS OF BATH (18TH CENTURY).

(From the sketch by Rowlandson.)

'Twas a glorious sight to behold the fair sex
All wading with gentlemen up to their necks,
And view them so prettily tumble and sprawl,
In a great smoking kettle as big as our hall.
And to-day many persons of rank and condition
Were boiled by command of an able physician.

THE EIGHTEENTH CENTURY

Fashionable Bath.

Several influences, early in the eighteenth century, led to the permanent rise of Bath from rowdyism and squalor to a proud position among England's fairest and most interesting cities. These influences were Fashion, the beneficent and beautifying enterprise of Ralph Allen, the architects Wood, senior and junior, and Beau Nash.

The general desire for cultivating Fashion seems to have had its origin in the eighteenth century. What the Court did and said and wore were themes for conversation and objects for imitation. Those not privileged to pass the august portals leading to the royal presence could take for their pattern the favoured few, and those whose aim was to follow the fashion, " stood gazing Court-wards in concentric circles."

Bath in the Eighteenth Century

was an important centre of fashion.

" Here met together all that was illustrious—the most noble ladies and the most celebrated men. The chiefs in every department, the heads and leaders of every movement, the foremost professors of every science, and the brightest ornaments of every art. The gamblers and duellists, those distinguishing characters of the age, made this their rendez-vous and battlefield. Players and playwrights, musicians, statesmen, theologians, philosophers, social reformers, Christian philanthropists—all muster in the same hour in the Pump Room, and mingle in the same crowd with idlers, ennui-dispellers and fortune-hunters. Hardly a biography, a memoir, or a novel of the eighteenth century, but contains some notice of Bath."

As fashion was the outcome of imitation, so was it necessary that the votaries of fashion should have recognized places of meeting, where objects and manners for imitation could freely be displayed. London society could be entered only by those who held a recognized public position. Provincial centres, whose lords were the local squires, were almost as exclusive. An independent social centre was needed whose doors no king could close, and into which no squire could forbid an entrance. Bath, already famous for its hot springs, and possessing good accommodation for visitors, became the rallying-place of good company.

The Academy of Fashion.

" The numbers who had come here for health only showed the way, whereupon the votaries of gaiety quickly made the place their own. Here was the seat, the garden, the playground, the parade of fashion. Forth from their agrarian homes came rustic squires at the instance of their wives and daughters, eager to learn the ways of ' good company,' and to be initiated into the mysteries of fashion."

Princess—afterwards Queen—Anne had been received at Bath and welcomed by the Corporation, much to the jealous displeasure of her sister, Queen Mary, who caused a letter of expostulation to be written to the Mayor of Bath.

The Mayor sent the letter to Mr. John Harington, of Kelston, the good friend and adviser in all that tended to the well-being of Bath ; and by his advice the matter was explained to the Princess, who good-naturedly desired the Mayor to allow her to be treated as a private visitor. In 1702 she came to Bath again, but this time received royal welcome as Queen.

The Renascence of Bath.

Queen Anne's visit was the foundation of Bath's prosperity as a fashionable centre. Visitors came in such numbers that at times the city could not entertain them all, and soon it was decided to extend the boundaries. The North and South Parades were built to the eastward, and still there was not accommodation for the crowds that flocked to drink the waters and to bask in the sunshine of fashion. The emergency made the man ; and the architect, Wood senior, came forward with his plans, to win for himself fortune and fame. "As a spirited speculator, and an architect who combined utility with elegance, Wood was qualified to stamp the architecture of a great city with the characteristics of solidity, utility, symmetry and space."

It was in 1728 that Wood began to build, and among his works Queen Square, Gay Street and the Circus are fitting memorials of his genius. Regions that were sinks of iniquity and dirt, and the resort of the rabble, he turned into graceful and stately thoroughfares that have won for Bath a place among the most beautiful cities of the Empire. He was also responsible for Ralph Allen's famous mansion at Prior Park. Wood senior was succeeded by Wood junior, " who surpassed all former magnificence of street architecture, and produced the most splendid and symmetrical object in Bath—the Royal Crescent."

The Makers of Modern Bath.

It is singular that so many writers persist in giving the title of the "maker" of England's most charming city to Beau Nash—the marshaller of fiddlers and dancers in the Assembly Rooms and the framer of laws for gamesters at the play tables. "It can scarcely be seriously considered," says Mr. Peach in his *Bath : Old and New*, "that any great city of the first rank in beauty and residential importance like Bath was danced and gambled into existence." It must be remembered that the so-called "reign" of Beau Nash synchronizes in great part with the lives of Ralph Allen, the city's best benefactor, and of the two Woods, the city's gifted rebuilders.

"Wood senior came to the city in 1727 at the instigation of Allen, who had already discovered the genius of the architect. Without Allen, Wood would have done little, with him, by him, and through him he could do everything. Allen had acquired the unworked quarries on Combe Down ; Wood understood, both scientifically and practically, the nature of the stone, and what it was capable of in the great building operations that he contemplated."

The Coming of Beau Nash.

Of importance in the establishment of Bath as a pleasure resort was the influence of Beau Nash, the famous Master of the Ceremonies. Richard Nash was born at Swansea, in 1674. From Carmarthen School he went to Jesus College, Oxford, but his ways did not commend themselves to the authorities. His departure was so hurried that he had no time to bid the bursar farewell ; and, in settlement of what was due to that functionary, he left behind a fiddle and a pair of boots, a tobacco box and a book of plays.

Then he entered the army ; but there were certain duties to be done in that profession, and he quickly doffed the red coat. His next move was to enter his name as a law student at the Middle Temple ; but the man of pleasure shrank from the drudgery of a legal training, and never became qualified. At the age of thirty he had no means, and no occupation, save that of a gamester.

HISTORIC BATH

The chronicles of the city record that in 1704 balls were given at the town hall, half a guinea being charged for a ticket; and the lesser gentry who patronized Bath considered half a guinea well expended in buying the opportunity of enjoying themselves in similar fashion with the great ones of the land. The ballroom and the gaming tables were thronged, and seats in the Bath coaches had to be booked several days in advance.

But the entertainments were lacking in refinement and organization. The ballroom reeked with tobacco smoke; men danced in muddy riding boots, the spurs of which worked mischief among many a feminine robe; and women, with a strange disregard of Court fashion which they desired to imitate, wore aprons as they danced. Lodgings were poor and dear; there were no good dining-rooms in the city; the Pump Room was a picture of disorder and squalor; and those who walked to their homes at night were certain to be insulted by the owners of the "Bath Chairs," who strove to make things uncomfortable for those who did not patronize them.

The Entrance of Beau Nash.

One day, in the midst of the dark age of Bath, a stage-coach rattled into the city, carrying as one of its passengers, a daintily dressed man whose name was Richard Nash. His manner and appearance pleased those who drank in the Pump Room and danced in the Town Hall; and soon his advice was sought and his word became law. He had no learning, his wit was poor, and his purse was empty. But scorned though he was by the great whose daily companion he soon became, there was genius of a kind in the man who could see at a glance the faults that clouded the future of Bath. The dormant energy that had not been roused by the glamour of Oxford and the legal possibilities of the Middle Temple was awakened by a sight of the chaos at Bath; and the man who could not make his own career set to work to help shape the fortunes of a city.

The Triumph of Beau Nash.

His first suggestions for improvement that would tempt the fashionable world to Bath were eagerly accepted; and soon, by popular accord, the direction of the affairs of the city was entrusted to him. Nash then became the uncrowned king of Bath, and his decisions were accepted as law. By his direction a permanent subscription list was established for the maintenance of a band and for keeping the Pump Room clean and in order; a fund was raised for paving and lighting the streets; and, in spite of Corporation opposition, the suburbs were improved, and a handsome Assembly Room built, surrounded by gardens. Here gaming could take place in the light of day, while cups of tea and chocolate were handed round.

Rules to be Observed at Bath.

In the Pump Room appeared a Code of Rules drawn up by Nash, as much for the exhibition of his own wit as for the regulation of Bath society. Some of the paragraphs are still interesting :—

" That no gentleman give his ticket for the balls to any but gentlemen. N.B.—Unless he has none of his acquaintance."

" That gentlemen crowding before the ladies at the ball show ill manners; and that none do so for the future, except such as respect nobody but themselves."

" That all repeaters of lies and scandals be shunned by all company, except such as have been guilty of the same crime."

It is recorded in the chronicles of Bath that all visitors, however high in rank, were bound to obey the laws of King Nash. When a nobleman once appeared among the dancers in riding boots, Nash is said to have reminded him that he had forgotten to bring his horse into the ballroom. He fixed the hour of eleven as the time for the closing of the evening dances; and once, when a royal princess appealed " for one dance more," he gravely bowed and assured her that the laws of Bath were as unalterable as those of the Medes and Persians.

Nash as a Social Reformer.

The carrying of swords was one of Beau Nash's pet aversions. They gave a distinguished appearance to the wearers; but when two visitors collided by accident, spoke hotly, and tragically met at moonlight in a Bath avenue, Nash drew up a new law to prevent such dangerous adornments, and the clashing of blades was henceforth never heard in the precincts of Bath. If a man dared to challenge another, he was promptly arrested; so strict was the rule of King Nash and so generally accepted both by people and authorities.

HISTORIC BATH

The Abbey Bells

were at Nash's suggestion brought into requisition as an item in Bath's social life. When a stage-coach rattled into the city with a batch of visitors, the newcomers would be greeted by the ringing of the bells; and, though invalids might complain, the practice gave satisfaction to the fashionable throng who, whether in the Pump Room or at home, in church or at the gaming table, would rush into the streets to inquire the names and position of the pilgrims. The ringers required a fee of half a guinea from the new arrivals.

These and other customs of Bath are pleasantly described by Christopher Anstey in his *New Bath Guide*, a collection of satires in rhyme that won for the author the honour of a memorial in Poet's Corner, Westminster Abbey.

" No city, dear mother, this city excels,
In charming sweet sounds, both of fiddles and bells;
I thought, like a fool, that they only would ring
For a wedding, or judge, or the birth of a king:
But I found 'twas for me that the good-natured people
Rang so hard, that I thought they would pull down the steeple.
So I took out my purse, as I hate to be shabby,
And paid all the men when they came from the Abbey.
Yet some think it strange they should make such a riot,
In a place where sick folk would be glad to be quiet;
But I hear 'tis the bus'ness of this corporation,
To welcome in all the great men of the nation."

A Day's Round in Bath.

There were three great daily functions in the fashionable circles of Bath—drinking the waters, attending the Abbey services, and putting in an appearance at the gaming tables. From six to nine were the bathing hours, followed by a leisurely drinking of the customary three glasses. Among the day's amusements were rides on horseback or by coach. " Some walk in the meadows round the town, winding along the side of the river Avon and the neighbouring canal, while others are seen scaling some of those romantic precipices that overhang the city." There were visits to pay and dinners to enjoy; another attendance to make at the Pump Room; and then the gay throng would pass into the grey old Abbey for the evening service, which was part of Fashion's routine. When the last Amen had been said, the congregation would look forward to the crowning delights of the day at the gaming tables and in the ballrooms.

BEAU NASH

The Zenith of Beau Nash.

" Nash was rewarded on all sides," says the chronicler, " with the smiles that wait on success and prosperity. The civic magistracy bowed to his royalty with the most flattering tokens of allegiance." He was at the height of his fame in 1738. The Prince of Orange presented him with a snuff-box, accompanied by complimentary words. Some of the nobility followed the example of royalty, and they were imitated by many of the gentry. His full-length picture was provided by public subscription and placed in Wiltshire's Ball Room between the busts of Newton and Pope. Of this occasion the cruel epigram, wrongly attributed to Lord Chesterfield, was penned by Jane Brereton :—

" Immortal Newton never spoke
   More truth than here you'll find ;
Nor Pope himself e'er penned a joke
   Severer on mankind.

" The picture placed the busts between
   Adds to the thought much strength ;
Wisdom and *Wit* are little seen,
   But *Folly's* at full length."

The Gaming Tables of Bath.

The position of Nash as Master of the Ceremonies was an honorary one ; by profession he was a gamester. Yet he was clever enough to make it appear that he had organized gambling only for the amusement of visitors. He was respected as a fair and honest gamester ; people spoke with admiration of his generosity to those who lost more than they could afford. Study had made him a good player, and had he possessed the cool callousness of most professional gamesters he might have won a fortune.

The Fall of Beau Nash.

Nash had never acted dishonestly as a gamester, and he expected honest treatment from the keepers of his gaming houses. They tricked him, and he called in the law to his assistance. From that moment his successful career was ended. It was revealed in evidence that, while he figured as the conductor of gaming tables in the interests of public amusement, he was growing rich as a sharer of the spoil. He lost both lawsuit and public esteem. Hosts of enemies appeared, " thick as gnats on the eve of a thunderstorm.'"

HISTORIC BATH

He was no longer the dazzling leader of a brilliant throng ; those who had only lately been his worshippers flung mud at him. It was for the first time seen, now that adversity had come upon him, that " Nature had by no means formed Mr. Nash for a Beau Garçon ; his person was clumsy, too large and awkward, and his features harsh, long, and peculiarly irregular. He had assiduity, flattery, fine clothes, and as much wit as the ladies he addressed."

The once brilliant leader of fashion, the maker of Bath's prosperity, was poor and friendless in his old age, and but for a humane grant of ten guineas monthly from the Corporation would have been a pauper. He died in St. John's Court, February 12, 1761, in his eighty-seventh year ; and in regard to his undoubted services to the city was given a public funeral in the Abbey. Even Anstey, the satirist, could in the *New Bath Guide* tinge his ridicule with praise of the man who had fallen :—

> " Long reign'd the great Nash, this omnipotent lord,
> Respected by youth and by parents ador'd :
> But alas ! he is gone, and the city can tell
> How in years and in glory lamented he fell ;
> Him mourn'd all the Dryads on Claverton's mount ;
> Him Avon deplor'd, him the nymph of the Fount.
> In reward of his labours, his virtues and pains,
> He is footing it now in the Elysian plains."

But the influence of Nash lived ; and Bath society, in its manners and arrangements, its follies and artificialities, remained for more than half a century much as it had been shaped by the great Master of the Ceremonies.

" But," wrote Mr. Traill, " while Nash was reforming the manners—certainly not the morals—of Bath, Ralph Allen was developing its industry, and Wood, under his encouragement, adorning the streets. It is mainly to Allen and the Woods that we owe all that is most characteristic in the existing city. The Pump Room and the baths, the Circus, the Crescent, and the Parades—it is about these that the spirit of the eighteenth century, those patch and powder days, chiefly seems to linger."

Mr. Pickwick in Bath.

Dickens, in the *Pickwick Papers*, pleasantly satirizes Bath society as it appeared early in the nineteenth century. Mr. Pickwick left the White Horse Cellar, Piccadilly, at 7.30 a.m., and reached the White Hart, in Bath, at 7 p.m. In

MR. PICKWICK IN BATH

a note on the subject Professor Earle tells us : " On the coach by which they travelled was remarked the name of Moses Pickwick. This is quite historical. There was a large coach proprietor of that name in Bath, and the name of Pickwick was conspicuous in the civic magistracy before the Municipal Reform Act."

Mr. Pickwick, who had come to Bath to regain health after the anxieties of the famous trial, was accompanied by his three bosom friends and the ever genial Sam Weller. The name of " Pickwick " on the coach disturbed Sam. He regarded it as a deliberately designed piece of impudence at the expense of his master. " How is that, Sam ? " " Why, the names is not only down on the vay-bill, sir, but they have painted vun of 'em up on the door of the coach."

" Angelo Cyrus Bantam, Esquire," who figures in the *Pickwick Papers* as Master of the Ceremonies, is thus pictured by Dickens :—

" A charming young man of not much more than fifty, dressed in a very bright blue coat with resplendent buttons, black trousers, and the thinnest possible pair of highly-polished boots. . . . His features were contracted with a perpetual smile, and his teeth were in such perfect order that it was difficult at a small distance to tell the real ones from the false.

" ' Welcome to Ba-ath, sir. This is indeed an acquisition. Most welcome to Ba-ath, sir. It is long, very long, Mr. Pickwick, since you drank the waters. It appears an age, Mr. Pickwick. Re-markable ! '

" ' It is a very long time since I drank the waters, certainly," replied Mr. Pickwick ; ' for to the best of my knowledge I was never here before.' "

Mr. Pickwick was fortunate enough to meet in the tea-room some distinguished members of Bath society, who were pointed out to him by the Master of the Ceremonies.

" ' Mr. Pickwick, do you see the lady in the gauze turban ? '

" ' The fat old lady ? ' inquired Mr. Pickwick, innocently.

" ' Hush, my dear sir—nobody's fat or old in Ba-ath. That's the Dowager Lady Snuphanuph.'

" ' Is it, indeed ? ' said Mr. Pickwick.

" ' No less a person, I assure you,' said the Master of the Ceremonies. ' Hush ! Draw a little nearer, Mr. Pickwick. You see the splendidly-dressed young man coming this way ? '

" ' The one with the long hair, and the particularly small forehead ? ' inquired Mr. Pickwick.

" ' The same. The richest young man in Ba-ath at this moment. Young Lord Mutanhead.'

" The card tables had to be visited before Mr. Pickwick could get within the inner ring of the most exclusive of Bath society.

" Poor Mr. Pickwick ! he had never played with three thorough-paced female card-players before. They were so desperately sharp that they quite frightened him. If he played a wrong card, Miss Bolo looked a small armoury of daggers ; if he stopped to consider which was the right one, Lady Snuphanuph would throw herself back in her chair, and smile with a mingled glance of impatience and pity to Mrs. Colonel Wagsby ; at which Mrs. Colonel Wagsby would shrug up her shoulders and cough, as much as to say she wondered whether he would ever begin. Then, at the end of every hand, Miss Bolo would inquire, with a dismal countenance and reproachful sigh, why Mr. Pickwick had not returned that diamond, or led the club, or roughed the spade, or finessed the heart, or led through the honour, or brought out the ace, or played up to the king, or some such thing ; and in reply to all these grave charges, Mr. Pickwick would be wholly unable to plead any justification whatever ; having by this time forgotten all about the game."

Jane Austen's Opinion of Bath.

The dawn of the nineteenth century marked the zenith of Bath's glory as a resort of fashion—particularly of the affectation of fashion. But the welcome decline was not far distant. The better class of visitors had grown weary of the artificial manners of the *beau monde* ; private parties were preferred to public amusements ; and in due course the Lower Assembly Rooms, the scene of Nash's triumphs, were advertised to be let. Jane Austen's novels, from 1809 to 1817, afford evidence of the poor opinion in which Bath society was then regarded by cultivated people. For their customs and opinions she openly expresses contempt, and gives dignity to her heroines by contrasting them with modish ladies of Bath. Queen Square was no longer regarded as the most exclusive residential situation. Says a character in Jane Austen's *Persuasion*, " I hope *we* shall be in Bath in the winter ; but remember, papa, we must be in a good situation—none of your Queen Squares for us ! "

Literary and Historic Associations.

The main interest of Bath in the last half of the eighteenth and in the first four decades of the nineteenth century had its source in the custom of leaders of intellectual life—painters and actors, novelists, poets and dramatists, statesmen and divines, explorers and warriors—to spend there a part of each year ; and it is this bright and fascinating era that lives in the comedies of Sheridan. There can be no doubt that Sheridan found at Bath the central idea of his *School for Scandal* ; for his early rough notes, still in existence, are headed thus : " The Slanderers : *A Pump Room Scene.*"

Of this golden age of Bath, Mr. Traill wrote :—

" It was during this period that Bath accumulated that mass of historic associations which give it among English cities a place only paralleled by that of the metropolis itself. Nowhere in England have so many of her greatest sons taken up at various times their abode, or left behind them such clear recollections of their sojourn. The names of Chatham and his yet greater son, of Burke and Camden, of Wolfe and Nelson, and Sir Sidney Smith, of Gainsborough and Lawrence, of Fielding, Goldsmith, Sheridan, Southey, Wordsworth, Jane Austen, Landor, may serve to illustrate without exhausting the list of notables—to most of whom Bath had been something more than a place of casual visit, either the actual birthplace or for long periods the home.

" The elder Pitt was for many years member for the city, and visited it at frequent intervals to obtain that relief from his famous malady which its waters never failed to afford. The comparative smallness of the place has made it possible to fix the exact abodes of nearly all the celebrities who have dwelt there ; and no other city, therefore, can show so remarkable a list of historic houses.

" It was at No. 7, Circus, that Pitt entertained General Wolfe on the eve of the latter's departure in command of the expedition to Quebec . . . and at No. 11, North Parade, that Edmund Burke spent four out of the last six years of his exhausted life, quitting it only to return home in order, as he said, to be ' nearer a habitation more permanent.' . . . The houses occupied by Nelson, by Goldsmith, and by Wordsworth can still be identified ; Lawrence was born there, and it was the birthplace of many famous pictures of Gainsborough, who, indeed, created during his residence there the reputation which he brought with him to London.

" Southey passed his boyhood at the house of his aunt, Miss Tyler, in Walcot, with a garden sloping down to the Avon bank. The memory of Sheridan's connection with the city will live as long as *The Rivals*, and so will that of Elizabeth Linley, famous in her own day for her beauty and her song, but better remembered in ours by the romance of Sheridan's courtship and marriage. The extent of Fielding's association with Bath—or rather the extent to which his romances reproduce the scenes and personages of the place—is, unfortunately, somewhat uncertain ; though loyal sons of Bath indeed will admit no uncertainty about it.

" To pursue further the literary associations of the city would take us to the days when Landor strode its Parades in his strange life-mood of defiant meditation, and when the strenuous idlers of Milsom Street were made to yield their humorous ' harvest ' to Jane Austen's quiet eye."

There are others that Mr. Traill might have included— men of letters like Pope and Warburton, Lytton and Dickens ; William Smith, the father of British geology ; actors of such repute as Quin, Garrick, and Mrs. Siddons ; philosophers like Berkeley and Butler ; and certainly should be remembered Herschel, who found time at Bath while acting as organist, as conductor of a band and organizer of concerts, to make telescopes and, after eighteen months' searching of the skies, to discover the planet *Uranus* in 1781.

The city annals tell us that two German princes, visitors at Bath, " honoured Mr. Herschel, organist of the Octagon Chapel, with their presence." Some might be inclined to put the honour in the other direction, considering that it was this humble organist who inspired Keats to the thought :

> " Then felt I like some watcher of the skies
> When a new planet swims into his ken."

The Growth of Modern Bath.

About 1830, Bath, while still a pleasure resort, was beginning to develop into the position it now holds as a permanent residential place. Attracted by the beautiful scenery, the mild climate and the numbers of well-built houses, generals and admirals of renown settled in Bath with their families ; and this dignified section of the population was in sharp contrast to the butterfly descendants of Beau Nash and his tribe. Bath was no longer, and never has been since that period, a fashionable resort alone. Indeed, so general a resort had it become that no thoroughfare out of London was so frequented as the great Bath Road ; nowhere else was the art of driving a coach carried to such perfection.

At last Bath was quite deserted by the class who had flocked thither to sit at the feet of Fashion, and its new life became more vigorous and prosperous than the old. In due course new streets stretched up the slopes of the neighbouring hills ; the beauty of the city was increased by gardens and parks ; stately hotels arose to meet the growing demand for accommodation ; and while thousands still flock to Bath for the sake of the healing waters, the city has become the permanent abode of a dignified and well-to-do community, attracted hither by interesting associations and a beautiful neighbourhood, by stately streets and crescents, and enchanting parks and gardens, that have won for the place the proud and well deserved title of " Queen of the West."

A Tribute to Bath.

Mr. Arthur Waugh in a recent article thus referred to Bath of the present and the past :—

" A city of the eighteenth century, bland and beautiful, dreaming with her grey stone eyes of the glories of an unforgettable past. Many of her mansions have known what it is to have shop fronts driven into their carved façades ; some of her chapels have changed into badminton courts and offices, and Beau Nash's private house is now a public theatre. But many more of the old buildings remain refreshingly unspoiled ; the link-extinguishers still survive amid the fine wrought-iron work ; the interiors, with their lofty, garlanded ceilings and noble doors, are still unsacrificed to vandalism. Indoors and out the city keeps its old-world face for those who have time to linger and to look for it, and nowhere more than in the long Assembly Rooms, where the towering chandeliers glitter with suggestion of ancient lights and the floor still shines from the polishing feet of the beaux and belles of a gayer generation.

" What a world one can call up, standing in the shadowy vestibule and looking down the dim and empty hall, what life and spirit of—

'The Old Augustan days
Of formal Courtesies and formal Phrase,
The Ruffle's Flutter and the Flash of Steel.'

Here Mrs. Malaprop grows garrulous over her cards ; there Lydia Languish's eyelashes lift in answer to some quick retort ; and surely that is Captain Absolute by the door, fresh and irresponsible as ever. Shadows of the past, flitting but imperishable ! "

THE STREETS OF BATH.

CHURCHES, parks and gardens, baths, antiquities, and residences of celebrities, are described in detail elsewhere ; and other useful information is set forth in alphabetical order in the preliminary section of this book. This chapter, therefore, is intended only to make the stranger familiar with the general aspect of the streets and the direction in which each leads.

FROM THE G.W.R. STATION TO THE ABBEY CHURCH.

To the left is Dorchester Street, out of which the third turning to the right leads by way of Southgate Street into the well-known thoroughfare of Stall Street. But we will ask our readers to enter Bath along **Manvers Street,** opposite the station. On the right hand is the traditional site of **King Bladud's Palace,** and a little beyond is the **Baptist Chapel.** On the left is Henry Street, with its Swedenborgian place of worship ; on the right, South Parade leads to the **Church and Priory of St. John the Evangelist,** one of the finest Roman Catholic structures in the kingdom. Manvers Street is continued by Pierrepont Street, at the end of which is the North Parade. At the corner, to the left, is the **Royal Literary and Scientific Institution.** Keeping this building to the right, we enter the once fashionable parade, **Terrace Walks,** at the end of which is **Orange Grove,** named in honour of the Prince of Orange. In the centre is an obelisk, bearing the inscription : " In memory of the happy restoration to health of the Prince of Orange, by drinking the Bath waters, through the favour of God, and to the joy of Britain, 1734." At the north-east corner is the large *Empire Hotel.* Westward of the Grove is the **Abbey Church** and adjoining it are the **Baths.**

TO AND FROM VICTORIA PARK.

North of the Abbey, at the corner of High Street, are the

Guildhall and the **New Municipal Buildings.** Northgate Street, a continuation of High Street, contains, in Northgate Chambers, the headquarters of the **Bath United Liberal Association ;** farther north, at the angle formed by the junction of Walcot Street with Broad Street, is **St. Michael's Church.** Passing to the right of the Church, along Walcot Street, we have on the right the **Corn and Cattle Market,** open on Saturdays ; north of that the name of the street changes to **Ladymead,** an association with the meadow which once occupied the site and sloped down to the river.

Ladymead in its turn gives place to **Cornwell Buildings,** the name being derived from Corn Well, a spring of cold mineral water which once rose in the vicinity, and was popular as an application to weak eyes. Passing the Penitentiary on the right, we reach, at the end of the road, **St. Swithin's Church,** the mother church of Walcot parish.

The street along which we have come is on the site of the Roman road known as the *Fosse ;* and if we turn sharply to the left, a few yards beyond the church, we have an equally famous Roman road, the *Via Julia,* now the **London Road.** On the right is **Hedgemead Park ;** on the left we pass a thoroughfare called the **Vineyards.** It was formerly part of a vineyard planted early in the seventeenth century and cultivated until 1730, when it was abandoned owing to the failure of the crops. The vines, trained on stakes, produced Black Cluster and Muscadine grapes, as many as sixty-nine hogsheads of wine having been made from them in one year.

On the west side of the Vineyards is the **Vineyards Chapel,** belonging to the Countess of Huntingdon's Connexion. John Wesley preached here in 1766, and on one occasion had Horace Walpole in his congregation. In the committee room adjoining the chapel are portraits of the Countess and of Rowland Hill and George Whitefield. At the end of this thoroughfare is the **Catholic Apostolic Church.** From the end of the Paragon, which faces the Countess of Huntingdon's Chapel, a flight of steps leads to Walcot Street.

Continuing our walk, by way of Guinea Lane, we cross the main thoroughfare and enter **Montpelier,** where we have on the right **Christ Church,** a district church of Walcot parish ; and a few yards beyond, on the same side of the road, is **St. Mary's Roman Catholic Church,** opened in 1781 to take the place of an earlier building. South of the chantry, which contains a beautiful stained window, and divided from it by a tastefully designed arcade, is the Chapel of the Sacred Heart.

Passing on to the junction of Harley Street with Julian Road, we see at the farther right corner **Portland Chapel,** dedicated to St. Augustine, and worthy of note if only because few other places of worship in the land have accommodated worshippers of so many different creeds. It was built by the Independents in 1816 ; was for some time a Roman Catholic Chapel, and in 1841 passed into the possession of the Church of England. On the opposite side of the road is **St. Andrew's Church ;** and just beyond is St. James' Street, leading into **St. James' Square,** the plain and massive houses of which date from 1790. In the centre of the Square is a well-kept lawn, about an acre in area. The site had previously been occupied by gardens, one plot being in the possession of the poet Anstey, who was inspired to many a pleasant rhyme while strolling among his favourite flower-beds. He received his notice to quit with no good will, and launched the following epigram upon those who had taken from him his pet garden :—

> " Ye men of Bath, who stately mansions rear,
> To wait for tenants from the de'il knows where,
> Would you pursue a plan which cannot fail,
> Erect a madhouse, and enlarge your jail."

At the north-west corner of the Square is Park Street, leading to **All Saints' Chapel,** where once ministered the eloquent Canon Fleming. Leaving the Square at the southwest corner, we soon reach **Victoria Park,** described on pp. 78–79. From the Park, by way of Marlborough Buildings, we approach the **Royal Crescent,** a stately and imposing row of thirty houses, built by Wood junior in 1769. The style is Ionic, with massive columns in front supporting a cornice of proportionate dimensions. Here lodged Mr. Pickwick, and here the unlucky Mr. Winkle, arrayed in his dressing gown, acted as night porter.

From the Crescent and the lawn in front fine views may be had of Victoria Park and the country beyond.

East of the Crescent is Brock Street, containing **Margaret Chapel,** opened in 1774 by the fashionable preacher, Dr. William Dodd, who was executed for forgery seven years later. It was used for a time for concerts and other entertainments, and is now a Presbyterian Church. Brock Street leads to **The Circus,** a circle of noble houses, begun in 1754 by Wood senior, and adorned with Doric, Ionic and Corinthian columns in successive tiers. Nearly opposite Brock Street is

THE STREETS OF BATH

Bennet Street, named in honour of Mr. Philip Bennet, who once represented Bath in Parliament. Here are the **Assembly Rooms.**

At the end of Bennet Street we turn to the right along Oxford Row, out of which a narrow thoroughfare on the left, Hay Hill, leads to **Hay Hill Baptist Chapel.** Oxford Row is continued by Fountain Buildings, and these again by Broad Street, where is **Jubilee Hall,** the local headquarters of the Young Men's Christian Association. Near this is the *York House Hotel*, one of the chief houses in the West of England in the old coaching days. In York Buildings, a turning to the right named in honour of the Duke of York, brother of George III, is the **General Post Office.** About the middle of Broad Street will be seen on the right **King Edward's School.** One of the most ancient thoroughfares of Bath is this **Broad Street,** inhabited in the sixteenth and seventeenth centuries by the local aristocracy, whose houses have now disappeared. The two oldest buildings are No. 35 and the *Saracen's Head*, which date respectively from 1709 and 1713. Out of this street Northgate Street leads into High Street, from which we started our walk.

A CIRCULAR WALK.

From the Abbey Churchyard turn west to **Union Street,** famous for its shops, and owing its name to the link it forms between Stall Street and Milsom Street. At the top of Union Street is the **Mineral Water Hospital,** where, opposite the new wing, may be seen a part of the old city wall surmounted by a modern battlement. From Union Street, within the old city boundaries, we pass, either by way of Old Bond Street or Burton Street, into Milsom Street, outside the ancient boundaries. Here is a building formerly known as the **Octagon Chapel,** but now serving—" to what base uses we may return ! "—as a warehouse. Here Dr. Magee, the eloquent divine who became Archbishop of York, was once incumbent ; and here, Herschel, the astronomer, acted as organist. It was during hi residence at Bath, when living at 13, New King Street, that Herschel made his name immortal by the discovery of the planet Uranus.

Milsom Street, the " Regent Street " of Bath, is lined by fine shops and other business buildings, including the principal banks. One of the most notable establishments is *Jolly's*, which has been frequented by the fashionable dames of Bath

and the surrounding district for upwards of a century. Facing
the top will be seen Edgar Buildings, where are the **Constitutional Club** and the **Church Institute.** At the top of Milsom
Street we turn to the left along George Street into **Gay Street,**
which leads on the right from George Street into the Circus,
and on the left to **Queen Square.** It is in the latter direction
that we would ask readers to accompany us. Queen Square,
built in 1729–35, was, until the Circus and Royal Crescent
were planned, the most fashionable residential quarter in
the city. Here lived for a time the then Prince of Wales, to
whose memory, on a lawn in the centre, stands an obelisk
with an inscription penned by Pope :—

" In memory of honours conferred, and in gratitude for benefits
bestowed on the city by His Royal Highness Frederick Prince of
Wales, in the year 1737. This obelisk is erected by Richard Nash,
Esq."

The **Bath and County Club** is at Nos. 21 and 22. From
the north-west corner of the Square we enter Charlotte Street,
on the left side of which is **Percy Congregational Chapel,** the
largest Nonconformist place of worship in Bath. Just beyond
is the beautiful **Moravian Chapel.** Leaving Charlotte Street
by the thoroughfare running southward by Percy Chapel, we
reach **St. Paul's Church ;** and by crossing Monmouth Place,
a continuation of Upper Bristol Road, and turning slightly
to the left, we enter Charles Street. Halfway down on the
right is New King Street, where stands the **Wesleyan Chapel,**
a fine structure opened by John Wesley in 1779, and rebuilt
in 1847. At the end of Charles Street, and facing it, is in the
wide thoroughfare of James Street, the **Joint Station** of the
Midland and the Somerset and Dorset Railways. It is one
of the largest stations in the West of England, and has a
tastefully designed frontage.

Turning to the left in James Street, and passing **Trinity
Church,** we bear to the left along New Street into **Kingsmead
Square.** Across the Square, directly opposite New Street,
is **Westgate Street,** out of which the first turning to the left
leads to **Saw Close,** which derives its name from having
formerly been used by sawyers. Here is held the Coal and
Hay Market ; and on the left is the *Garrick's Head,* for some
years the residence of Nash, next door to it being the house
where he died. Close by is the **Theatre.** Leading out of
Saw Close on the right is the thoroughfare known as Borough

Walls, in which is the **Blue Coat School,** a modern building in the Elizabethan style.

Returning to the Kingsmead Square end of Westgate Street, crossing the road and passing up Westgate Buildings, we reach, at the end of this thoroughfare, the site of the old **West Gate,** a wing of which, demolished in 1776 for convenience of traffic, was frequently used as a residence for royal visitors to Bath. In Westgate Buildings are situated the **Primitive Methodist Chapel,** rebuilt in 1866 ; **Chandos House,** a large structure in which the Petty Sessions were once held ; and, a few yards beyond, the **Abbey Church House,** which formerly bore the name of **Hetling House.** It was built in 1572 by Sir Walter Hungerford, during the reign of Queen Elizabeth, was occupied in 1746 by Princess Caroline and her sister, the Princess of Wales, and still retains a stately fireplace with other relics of its past grandeur. This ancient mansion was the scene of much splendid hospitality in the time of the Stuarts ; and for centuries the most famous visitors to Bath were entertained within its walls. Royalty frequently visited Hetling House. At the end of Westgate Buildings we have on the left Hot Bath Street, leading to the **Baths,** adjoining the Cross Bath being **St. John's Hospital,** facing Bath Street. At the corner of Hot Bath Street and Lower Borough Walls, a thoroughfare owing its name to the fact that it runs along the city's ancient boundary, is the **Royal United Hospital ;** and half-way down Lower Borough Walls is the old burial-ground of St. James', now planted with flowers and evergreens. Lower down we come to the meeting-place of Southgate Street and Stall Street, southern portions of the great thoroughfare passing from south to north of Bath, and continued by Union Street and Milsom Street.

THE HOT SPRINGS.

Hours of Opening.—WEEK DAYS.—King's and Queen's Baths, New Royal Baths and Old Royal Baths, 7 a.m. to 7 p.m. Grand Pump Room, 8 a.m. to 6 p.m.

The Bathing Establishments may be viewed between 1 p.m. and 3 p.m.

SUNDAYS.—King's and Queen's Baths, New Royal Baths and Old Royal Baths, 7 a.m. to 9.30 a.m. Grand Pump Room, 12.15 p.m. to 1.30 p.m.

From October 1 to March 31 all Baths are open at 8 a.m.

EIGHTEEN hundred years ago the Romans, who appreciated the virtue of water, saw the hot springs bubbling from the ground at Bath, tasted them, bathed in them, and forthwith founded a city around them. Here they built stately temples and villas, made baths in which to wash and fountains from which to drink ; and, as we have shown, the foundations of their work endure to this day.

For untold centuries the springs have poured forth their healing waters ; their volume of half a million gallons daily has never varied, nor has their temperature changed even by the fraction of a degree. Such consistency of supply and temperature, uninfluenced by wet or dry seasons, hot or cold weather, affords proof beyond question that the source must be at a very great depth, and the area a vast one which has fed through the ages these springs of Bath.

The Origin of the Hot Springs.

Microscopic examination has shown that the sands brought up by the waters from the bowels of the earth " contain fragments of minute sea-urchins and sea-spiders, the latter resembling the claws of tiny crustaceæ ; also little bits of shells, and pieces suggestive of compound molluscs." Thus it is certain that the sources of the springs have connexion in some way with the sea.

The same microscopic examination has further proved that the heat of the waters is derived from a volcanic source.

THE HOT SPRINGS

A part of the deposited sand was seen to be pieces of lava similar to that found on the slopes of Vesuvius.

"Blistered and bubble-blown," wrote the late Mr. J. W. Morris, who made the observations we are noting, "these fragments often contain pieces of quartz, clasped and imprisoned by the molten metal as it cooled, precisely as the coins deposited by the enterprising visitor are clasped by the cooling lava of our volcanoes."

The three springs have a common origin, but the outlets are perfectly distinct, though close together, the temperature differing only 3 degrees from that of the hottest spring, which is 120°F.

The geology of Bath indicates that at some time a great volcanic convulsion and upheaval happened. This would account for the fact of the junction of two different geological formations in Bath, a fact which is invariably concurrent with the existence of hot springs. Judging, says the *Lancet*, from the beautiful specimens in the collection of Mr. Morris, there is evidence of some connexion with marine sources. The waters evidently course through long fissures, and on their way probably come into contact with coal measures, for particles of coal are occasionally thrown up by the bubbling waters.

An Analysis of the Waters.

The following analysis was made at the *Lancet* laboratory :—

	Grains per gallon.
Calcium sulphate	102·880
Strontium sulphate	2·030
Sodium sulphate	23·500
Potassium sulphate	0·207
Calcium carbonate	8·750
Magnesium chloride	15·800
Sodium chloride	9·080
Lithium chloride	0·120
Silica	1·960
Bromine	Traces.
Nitrates	None.
Carbonate of iron	1·600
	165·927

The walls of the baths give evidence of an important iron constituent of the waters. Spectroscopic analysis shows lithium clearly, and also strontium, and bromine is just detectable.

RADIUM IN BATH

The Three Thermal Springs.

The hot waters arise from three separate springs, close together, and are all included in one well-built, luxurious group of establishments known as the **Baths of Bath.**

I.   The " **King's Bath** " **Spring.**—This is the historic bath spring from which, probably, the Romans derived their supply. It was excavated by the late Major Davis, the terraces and columns being in a wonderful state of preservation. A view of the spring, throwing up water at the rate of 2½ hogsheads per minute, and overflowing in the centre of the " King's Bath," may be seen from a south window in the Grand Pump Room. The temperature is 117° F.

II.   The " **Hot Spring.**"—This rises 17 ft. below the pavement of the Old Royal Baths, and throws up water with a temperature of 120° F. at the rate of 1½ hogsheads per minute.

III.   The " **Cross Bath** " **Spring.**—This rises 15 ft. below the bath flooring, has a temperature of 114° F., with a supply of about half a hogshead per minute.

Radium in Bath.

The healing virtues of the hot springs of Bath have been known for very many centuries ; but it is only in the present day that the reason for cures that have approached the miraculous has been found in the presence of radium.

It is curious to note, writes an authority on the subject, that the ordinary analysis of the gases of the Bath waters failed to give any clue concerning the mystery of their extraordinary efficacy, except in the traces detected of helium. It was left to Sir William Ramsay to startle the scientific world in 1903 by the discovery that the existence of helium is proof positive of the presence therein of radium, because helium is the product of radium, being evolved after decomposition.

Radium not an Element.

Radium is composed of two elements, *helium* and *niton*, and while it is releasing helium it is also setting free the other and far more valuable essence—niton. One is practically useless from the point of view of medicine ; the other, niton, is of the highest value. There is no other spa in England, or abroad, which has so generous a proportion of the vitalizing niton evolved from radium as Bath. Whatever be the chosen

THE WATERS

means by which the healing powers of radium shall be harnessed and directed, Bath will be to the front in organizing and employing this marvellous force. The city is veritably a radium bath. The waters of the springs are not alone in giving forth exhalations of the life-restoring essence. The glasses from which the niton-charged waters are drunk become slowly stained a deep amber yellow ; and with this radio-active essence Bath is permeated. That she will turn to the best possible account the healing gifts so lavishly conferred by Nature none can doubt who know with what enterprise and ability the beautiful city is governed.

These important scientific discoveries have been followed by the addition of new methods of applying the waters in the cure of disease. Apparatus has been installed whereby the natural radio-active waters of the Hot Springs may be inhaled, or used for special sprays, in a finely atomized form. In suitable cases the gases from the springs, rich in radium emanation, are applied in conjunction with the water.

The Waters as Medicine.

The characteristics of the waters, from the medicinal view, are the sulphates of the alkalies and alkaline earths, together with the salts of magnesium and sodium, and they have a distinct action as a solvent of uric acid. Experiments have shown that Bath water dissolves over five times the amount of uric acid that distilled water would similarly take up at blood heat. Since the waters are drunk hot and used hot for bathing purposes, this fact doubtless has an important relation to their curative value in the treatment of chronic gouty affections and rheumatism.

The water is clear and sparkling, without odour, and with a very slight saline chalybeate taste which is not unpleasant ; and it does not excite the nausea which in many cases attends the drinking of ordinary hot water. Although colourless, the water tinges the glasses in which it is served, an action not due to iron, as was once supposed, but, according to an official statement made by Sir William Ramsay, to the presence of radium. The quantity to be taken is, of course, regulated by the physician. As a rule, from half a pint to a pint and a half is ordered daily, and this amount should regulate the system by washing out the stomach and intestines and flushing the kidneys. The beneficial action brought out by this natural lavage is most marked in cases of gout and chronic gastric affections.

In certain forms of disease the Bath waters have been most useful when taken cold. In cases of cystitis the results are very encouraging ; and here it may be mentioned that the waters are artificially aërated and sold under the name of *Sulis Water*, which forms a palatable table water. Another peculiarity is that if a patient is unable to take iodide of potassium in the ordinary way, it can be drunk without trouble when added to the Bath waters.

Open-Air Drinking.

Drinking the waters in the open-air has always been recognized as one of the enjoyable features of Continental Spas which English health-resorts have been slow to adopt. A welcome addition to the attractions of Bath, and a great movement forward in the direction of the city's future as a summer resort, was the opening on July 10, 1909, of the **Hot Mineral Water Fountain,** under the Colonnade in the beautiful Institution Gardens. Here the summer-cure visitor may sip the waters amid pleasant surroundings, listening the while to band-music. By the opening of the Colonnade and Fountain and the provision of music in the Gardens, the Corporation have wisely turned the routine of water-sipping into an alluring out-of-door amusement ; and the Gardens are one of the most popular rendezvous of visitors during the spring and summer seasons.

Diseases treated by the Waters.

Gout.—Not every patient afflicted with this complaint, we learn from the *Lancet*, will benefit by a visit to Bath, but the majority will ; and those who have unsuccessfully tried other English and Continental spas need not be discouraged on that account from trying a course of the Bath thermal waters. Dr. Luff, in his *Gout : its Pathology and Treatment*, points out that sodium salts act against the removal of gouty deposits, and that only those springs are suitable which contain none, or only traces, of such salts. Under such category the Bath waters may be classed ; hence their unique value in the treatment of gout.

Of benefit, too, are the waters in removing or relieving disorders related to gout, such as gastric irregularities, gastric and intestinal catarrh, acidity, constipation, portal congestion and certain urinary disorders. Much may be done in the way of massage, and in the use of the baths and douches,

ALCOVE IN THE PUMP ROOM.   COOLING ROOM, QUEEN'S BATH.   CONCERT ROOM, ROMAN PROMENADE.

THE GRAND PUMP ROOM.

to remedy the inflammatory thickening of the tissues, articular stiffness, contraction of tendons, etc. In gouty dyspepsia the waters should be sipped at a temperature of 117° or higher, beginning with a small dose and rapidly increasing it. For the more chronic forms there are, in addition to the vapour baths, the deep and reclining baths and the douches ; and relief is found in the massage bath when carefully used under express advice. When treatment is followed by an acute attack of gout, relief has been afforded by the Berthollet vapour bath. No doubt exists as to the general benefit of the Bath waters in such cases ; but much depends on the accompanying careful dieting, and adherence to the physiological righteousness enforced by medical advisers.

Chronic Rheumatism.—Satisfactory results have followed, especially in cases of patients convalescent after acute or sub-acute attacks. The waters are employed warm, locally or generally, either in the deep or reclining bath when the patient is weak ; and when he is stronger, the Aix massage, hot douching and vapour baths are used with massage and active and passive movements. The waters are noted, in these cases, for their soothing effects and the alleviation of pain. The massage given while in the bath has a strong effect in making pliable thick and stiffened joints. Vapour baths are used to cause perspiration, to aid absorption and soften the joint tissues. Muscular rheumatism will, as a rule, require the Aix massage douche, together with dry massage ; and if these methods do not give relief, first the Berthollet vapour bath, and then the massage reclining bath, are tried.

Sciatica.—Local physicians speak well of the relief often obtained from the deep baths with undercurrent douche ; but only the simple bath can be used in acute cases.

Digestive Disorders.—Dyspepsia, constipation and flatulence are very frequently relieved when patients will submit to the dietetic regulations, as well as keep the stomach washed by drinking the waters, and take the prescribed baths combined with massage. Muco-membranous colitis and similar conditions are successfully treated by intestinal douching. The radio-active mineral waters have proved of great value in the relief of these obstinate diseases.

Skin Diseases.—Eczema and other diseases of the skin are successfully treated at Bath, the results being particularly good when the trouble is of a rheumatic or gouty origin. Reclining tepid baths are generally first employed, and from day to day the temperature of the water and the duration of immersion are gradually increased.

Nervous Diseases.—Chorea is successfully treated at Bath, especially when it has a rheumatic origin ; and equally so are the various forms of peripheral neuritis.

THE HOT SPRINGS

Respiratory Diseases.—For chronic bronchitis, chronic laryngitis and pharyngitis the water is used in a pulverized form ; but the results are almost invariably best when the trouble is dependent upon a gouty constitution.

Results of Injury.—Stiffness and pain, as the results of injury to joints, are greatly relieved by the douches and massage.

Debility.—Convalescence after protracted disease, or after acute affections, may be accelerated by a course of treatment at Bath.

The complaints we have briefly indicated as being successfully treated at Bath might be added to almost indefinitely. But the sufferer can only be vaguely pointed the way by the suggestions to which we have been helped by the pages of the *Lancet*. The consulting physician, who looks into each case, alone can judge what course is best for the individual.

In justice it may be added that the attendants at the baths are intelligent and earnest, and have so strong a belief in the efficacy of the baths and their own capabilities that they take with brisk hopefulness the most down-hearted patient submitted to them. " If you know any one," said a bath attendant to the writer, " who has been given up as a hopeless case elsewhere, send him to *me*." There was a wealth of confidence in the " *me* " which would have made a patient who heard it look forward to a near day when he could skip up Beechen Cliff and happily survey the beautiful city in whose waters he had been healed.

The Volume of the Springs.

From a statement issued by authority of the Corporation we learn that the water for the baths is forced by means of two pumps into a high, closed tank, that can hold 20,000 gallons. The pumps are each capable of dealing with that amount of water per hour, so that a plentiful supply is assured under considerable pressure. The consumption for the various baths is enormous. The single baths generally contain 780 gallons, and the largest single baths 900 gallons.

Close upon a thousand different taps are employed to serve the establishment ; their connecting pipes would, if extended continuously, make a length of forty miles. The abundance of water is enough not only to supply fresh mineral water to each individual bather, but also the baths of the various free hospitals.

GRAND PUMP ROOM

Bathing tickets must in all cases be procured from the office adjoining the Grand Pump Room, Abbey Churchyard. It is always advisable to book appointments for baths well in advance. The scale of charges for the various classes of baths can be obtained on application.

Visitors' Tickets.

These tickets, sold at the Inquiry Office at the rate of 4s. weekly, 6s. 6d. fortnightly, and 10s. 6d. monthly, entitle the holders to admission to the Pump Room, the Roman Promenade, with the use of the drawing-room, smoking-room, etc., and the Roman Baths, as well as to the Institution Gardens, Sydney Gardens, and the Royal Victoria Park. They also allow the free use of a chair in any of these places.

Ticket holders have admission to the ordinary concerts and symphony concerts given by the Pump Room Orchestra, to band performances in the gardens and parks, and to frequent special fêtes and entertainments.

The ticket also frees the holder from all charges for the drinking of the mineral waters, and, among other privileges, includes reduced charges for boat hire on the Avon.

Visitors, however, who prefer to pay the single charge for admission are at liberty to do so.

The centre of Bath's bathing and social system is—

The Grand Pump Room.

at the south-west corner of the Abbey churchyard. It was erected in 1796 on the site of the structure in which Beau Nash had ruled as Master of the Ceremonies. The main feature of the exterior consists of a façade with four Corinthian pillars supporting a pediment, on the frieze of which is the motto, in letters of gold—ΑΡΙΣΤΟΝ ΜΕΝ ΥΔΩΡ (" Water indeed is best "), quoted from the first ode of Pindar and freely rendered by Sir William Boyd—

> " Chief of Nature's works divine,
> Water claims the highest praise."

The *Pump Room* is intended by the Corporation, to whom the Baths belong, to be used by the ordinary visitor as well as by those who have come to use the waters. It is a large, lofty, stately room, luxuriously furnished and beautifully decorated. For over a century visitors have daily assembled here to chat, read, lounge and drink from the spring, or not drink from it, as necessity or inclination dictate.

GRAND PUMP ROOM

At each end of the Pump Room is a recess, one of which contains a *Statue of Beau Nash*. Opposite the principal entrance is an **Alcove** of extremely beautiful design, divided from the hall of the Pump Room by a bar, behind which the "neat-handed Phyllis" dispenses draughts of Bath waters from a fountain directly supplied by the King's Bath spring. This lovely alcove is adorned with a marble statue by James Barrington Ward, representing the angel descending to trouble the healing pool of Bethesda (*St. John* v. 4). It is a duplicate of that in the Walker Art Gallery, at Liverpool.

The windows of the alcove are of stained glass, picturing events of special interest to Bath—Bladud and the Swine, Roman Soldiers, the Coronation of King Edgar, the Visit of Queen Elizabeth, and the Entry of Queen Anne.

In the Annexe known as the **Roman Promenade**, opened in 1897, are exhibited numerous and valuable relics of a past civilization, recovered from time to time during excavations upon the site of the Roman Thermæ.

The Roman Promenade is on the eastern side of the Pump Room, and connected with it are a smoking room, a ladies' parlour, a cloak room, and in the basement a museum. Afternoons may be spent amidst these pleasant surroundings, listening to music provided by one of the finest orchestras in England. The daily concerts and weekly symphony performances have made the Roman Promenade a favourite resort of music lovers. The season here of the City Orchestra is from October to May.

This new Roman Annexe hides nothing of the old work. It is so constructed that "while preserving the antiquities from exposure to the weather, it affords opportunity for an enjoyment and study of those wonderfully preserved evidences of a former magnificence, with every facility of access and comfort. The Promenade has proved a great convenience to visitors during the winter season, affording as it does all the comforts and conveniences of a private club. It is rendered attractive by the best music, the talented orchestra being famed for its musical perfection ; and visitors have the opportunity of subscribing for weekly, monthly or annual tickets at reduced rates. The terraces afford accommodation for dispensing light refreshments and for promenading ; while, in summer time, delightful shade is found below on the Roman scholæ."

Adjoining the grand Pump Room is—

THE GREAT ROMAN BATH.

THE CIRCULAR ROMAN BATH.

A. F. Perren,] ENTRANCE TO THE KING'S BATH. [Bath.

THE KING'S BATH.

The King's Bath,

familiar in local pictures and literature of the eighteenth century. It is said to derive its name from King Bladud, the legendary founder of the city; and certainly it is the oldest bath. Fifty-nine feet in length, and in breadth 40 feet, it takes eleven hours to fill. The visitor may, at any time, see the water bubbling up through a stone well.

The *Queen's Bath*, the name of which is now merged in the King's Bath, was originally provided for the use of the poor. It was removed in 1886 to expose to view the **Circular Roman Bath** beneath it.

The New Portion,

reached by a passage from the King's Bath entrance, was added between 1886 and 1889 at a cost of £20,000, with the result of making the establishment equal in comfort, style and efficiency to the best Continental spas. On three sides of the beautiful central hall used as a cooling room are entrances to baths and dressing-rooms; and on the fourth side are stained windows, one of which pictures the three Emperors of Rome—Vespasian, Titus and Constantine—who were concerned in the foundation of the baths 2,000 years ago. In the centre is the inscription—

> "The spring from whence these waters flow
> In the deep rock lies hid below,
> So let thy bounty hidden be,
> And only God the giving see."

The baths, to which access is obtained from this central hall, are freely open to inspection at stated hours, except, of course, when in use. They include the most modern and scientific appliances, are beautifully tiled and furnished, and should certainly be seen, for they are among the most interesting of the sights of Bath. The visitor, too, will be pleased with the courtesy and intelligence of the attendants.

On the front of this building are three tablets with inscriptions, in the following order :—

" These Hot Springs were used by the Romans as early as the first century. In area, in grandeur, in completeness, the Baths of Aquæ Sulis were unequalled. The remains of their magnificence are here disclosed.

" These Healing Waters have flowed on from time undated to this day. Their virtue unimpaired; Their volume unabated; Their heat undiminished. They explain the origin

THE ROMAN BATHS

account for the progress, and demand the gratitude of the City of Bath.

"This extension of the King's and Queen's Baths, continuing the usefulness and developing the advantages of the Mineral Springs, was completed in the Mayoralty of Henry William Freeman, and graciously opened June xiii., MDCCCLXXXIX., by her Royal Highness, Helen, Duchess of Albany. C. E. Davis, F.S.A., Arch."

Adjoining the Grand Pump Room and the Roman Promenade is the Central **Ticket Office,** where all arrangements are made for baths. The office of the Director of the Baths is also here.

An **Inquiry Office** forms part of the facilities organized here for the convenience of visitors. Information on all subjects of interest to strangers is gladly given free of cost.

Visitors' Tickets are obtained here.

From the main entrance to the Grand Pump Room and Roman Promenade access is gained to—

The Roman Baths.

Some of the remains were brought to light in 1755, thirty feet below the surface, and covered again. In 1883 more remains were unearthed, and the work of excavation was then taken up by the Corporation.

The **Rectangular Bath** is situated in the centre of a hall 111 feet long by 68½ feet wide. Encircling it is a stone platform, nearly 14 feet wide, with six steps leading to the water. On both sides are seat recesses, and around are stumps of the stone piers which supported the roof arches. Some of the wedge-shaped hollow bricks that composed the arches are still to be seen, as are portions of the lead pipe which conducted the water from the spring to the bath. The **Circular Bath,** with a diameter of 29 feet, is situated beneath the new buildings. The **Thermæ,** corresponding somewhat to our modern Turkish baths, still show the heating chambers in a good state of preservation.

To view the modern baths in order, we must return to Stall Street, and take in turn the series of baths fed by the King's Bath Spring. Of these, the most important are—

The New Royal Baths,

opposite the Colonnade. They were built in 1870 by the Corporation at an expense of £12,000. The entrance hall opens into a corridor 200 feet long, with approaches on each side to the different baths. Among these are several deep baths fitted with jets for applying the wet douche, dry douche baths, two large reclining baths, and Aix massage with powerful needle douche. Plombières douches are given in this building ; also the Dowsing radiant heat and light treatment.

The **Swimming Bath,** 80 feet long by 35 feet wide, is approached by steps at the end of the corridor, and has another entrance in St. Michael's Place. Its capacity is 40,000 gallons, renewed daily from the King's Bath Spring, and the temperature is about 84°. At one end of the room is the *Wood Nymph Statue*, the last work of Joshua Wall, who carved the lions at the entrance to the hotel. In addition to dressing rooms attached to the various baths there are pleasant apartments, one for ladies and the other for gentlemen, in which bathers may cool themselves after their dip ; and there is also a smoking-room. Instructors are in attendance to give lessons in swimming. On Mondays and Fridays the swimming bath is set apart for the use of ladies. On the same floor is a douche massage room in which can be had the Aix massage, dry douche, needle bath, sitz bath, spinal and reclining bath. Oxygen baths are also employed in suitable cases.

The **Thermal Soolbäd,** for the treatment of cardiac cases by the application of carbonic acid gas on the Nauheim system, is largely given here.

The **Electric Hot Air Bath,** on the Greville system, is another up-to-date addition in connection with the King's Bath. The treatment can be applied either locally or to the whole body ; free perspiration is produced ; and, in consequence, the body temperature is increased, the blood circulates more freely, and the poisonous matter which has caused the trouble is eliminated through skin and kidneys.

The **Public Hot Water Fountain** is at the east end of Bath Street, a thoroughfare whose piazza on each side is a link between the days of the architects Wood and our own.

The Hetling, or Hot, Spring supplies the **Old Royal Private Baths,** comprising numerous baths, some holding about 800 gallons. One of them is furnished with a crane, to which is attached an armchair in which an invalid, incapable of self-action, may sit and be lowered into the water. Shower, reclining and other baths are numbered among the conveniences offered to visitors by the " Old Royal." The dressing rooms are warm, lofty, well lighted and comfortable, and the tedium of the " cooling-rooms " is lessened by a supply of periodical literature. The **Hetling Pump Room** provides water for drinking at the natural temperature of the spring, or, if necessary, super-heated to 150°, to meet the requirements of medical men.

The **Tepid Swimming Bath,** built in 1829, adjoining the " Old Royal," and supplied by the Hetling Spring, is 62 feet in length and 23 feet in breadth. It is for gentlemen only, and the fees are lower than at the " New Royal." What is known as the **Hot Bath** is set apart for the poor, to whom tickets are given ; and the **Cross Bath** is a cheap public bath.

Appliances in Use at the Baths.

(Medical advice should always be taken before using the Baths.)

The baths are under Corporation management ; but with regard to apparatus and appliances the advice of a specially-appointed committee of medical men is followed. No matter what the cost of a new method of treatment, or of an improvement on one already adopted, it is certain to be added if advised by the Committee.

The Deep or Chair Bath.—Each of these T-shaped baths holds from 800 to 900 gallons, and has an average depth of 4 feet 6 inches. It is large enough to permit free movement, is lined with porcelain slabs, and provided with marble seats. For those patients who cannot walk into the bath, there is a wooden armchair suspended from a metal rail. By pulleys the chair is brought to the dressing room, drawn over the bath and gently lowered by easily controlled hydraulic power into the water. A special feature here is the " under-current douche," consisting of a hose and nozzle, which applies to the patient's body a powerful stream whilst under water.

The Reclining Baths.—These are for patients unable to use the deep baths, and are fitted with appliances for the " under-current douche."

Aix Massage Douche Baths.—Each douche room—as in the Aix-les-Bains system—has two or three dressing rooms, to save delay through waiting. Care is taken in regulating the temperature, and chairs and stools are sprayed with hot water before being used. While the bath is being taken the floor is covered with 4 inches of water, the excess running off into the Roman culvert. During the application of massage the patient is douched with water at the stipulated temperature, which, towards the end of the treatment, is

THE GRAND PUMP ROOM AND ABBEY CHURCH.

HIGH STREET AND THE GUILDHALL.

BATH ABBEY.

THE WEST DOOR.

gradually lowered; and finally comes the cool shower or needle bath. Then the patient returns to the dressing room to be "packed," and to grow cool in a comfortable room supplied with literature.

Vichy Douche- Massage.—In this treatment the patient lies in a recumbent position on an india-rubber air mattress while massage is given under a series of fine spray douches. If desired, jets or wave douches may be substituted for the sprays. The massage is followed by direct douching.

Needle Bath.—This apparatus, which sprays the whole of the body at the same time, is noted for the extremely bracing effect it produces.

The Local Spray.—This is known as the "dry douche," and is used in cases where it is not well for the patient to bathe. A strong current of water at a temperature of 115° is sprayed over the part affected, the rest of the body being kept dry. It is not even necessary for the patient to undress. The method is very efficacious in chronic joint trouble.

The Scottish Douche.—This is used in the douche-massage room, and consists of two hoses by which strong streams of hot and cold water alternately are played on the body.

Sitz Bath.—By means of this system sprays or streams of water can be thrown in the desired direction according to the tap which is turned. It has proved useful as a lumbar spray or spinal bath, or as an enema bath.

Plombières Douches.—The treatment consists of an internal douche of mineral water followed, in most cases, by a reclining bath with a special form of under-current douche known as the Tivoli douche. The radio-active mineral waters of Bath are specially suitable for this treatment. Cases of colitis, muco-membranous colitis, chronic constipation, and some other diseases derive marked benefit from a course of these douches.

Berthollet, or Natural Vapour Baths.—These can be applied either generally or locally. By means of an ingenious contrivance any part of the body can be brought under the influence of steam from the thermal waters. In cases of acute gout the pain is lessened and the attacks shortened. For general application the patient is seated in a wooden box, and, with the exception of his head, is entirely shut in. Some sub-acute and chronic forms of eczema have been greatly relieved by the free perspiration that ensues from this natural vapour treatment.

Medicated Baths are employed by the addition of sulphur, pine, bran, oatmeal, etc., to the thermal waters. The Sulphur Bath is frequently used in cases of skin disease.

Electric Hydro Bath.—Electricity is applied to the body when in the water, and immediate relief given in cases of joint and muscle pains, neuralgia and kindred troubles. **Dowsing Radiant Light and Heat Treatment.**—This valuable therapeutic method is one of the most recent installations, and may be obtained at the Bathing Establishment, followed, where so ordered, by douches of the natural mineral water.

Electric Hot Air Baths.—The Greville System has proved of great value in cases of stubborn rheumatism or gout and is regarded by the medical profession as one of the safest in existence for applying dry heat. The generators are of various sizes and shapes, being designed for application upon only that part of the body affected.

The Zander Institute.

One of the most important of modern additions to the Hot Mineral Baths of Bath has been made by the installation of apparatus for medico-mechanical treatment at the recently opened Zander Institute, adjoining the New Royal Baths.

This treatment consists of methods for strengthening and controlling muscular action by means of mechanical appliances designed by Dr. Zander, of Stockholm.

In connection with the mineral water cure the methods have been of great value in cases of stiffened joints, rheumatism, etc. ; and have proved highly successful in the cases of boys and girls suffering from general weakness.

THE CHURCHES OF BATH.

THE most imposing architectural feature of Bath is—

The Abbey Church,

prominently situated in the centre of the city. It ranks as the latest example on a large scale in England of Perpendicular work. The present building was begun in the reign of Henry VII by Oliver King, Bishop of Bath and Wells, on the site of a Saxon nunnery. After a time a monastery founded by Offa, King of Mercia, took the place of this nunnery, and during the Norman period it was annexed to the bishopric of Wells. John de Villula, the then Bishop of Wells, deciding to have his throne in Bath, swept away the old Saxon Church and began the building of a Norman structure. Fifteen years later Bath was ravaged by fire, and out of the fragments of Villula's church a still larger and more beautiful building was erected. Of this Norman structure traces may be seen at the east end exterior of the present Abbey in the shape of two pier bases.

Bishop King's Dream.

For three centuries the church stood; but it had become so ruinous through neglect that rebuilding was absolutely necessary. It is a pleasant story that is told of Bishop Oliver King, who went to Bath in 1499 to institute Prior Birde into his office. In a dream he saw, beneath the figure of the Divine Majesty, a ladder with angels ascending and descending, while at the foot was an olive tree supporting a crown. In the dream he seemed to hear the words, " Let an *Olive* establish the Crown, and let a *King* restore the Church."

The Bishop lost no time in starting the building of a new church; and the greater part of the present Abbey was erected before his death in 1503. The west front, which pictures in sculpture the dream of Bishop King, has some ludicrous features, for one or two of the angels seem to be falling headlong instead of gracefully descending ; but the whole work, properly regarded, is pleasing and one of the most singular pieces of architecture in existence.

At the suppression of the monasteries, evil times befell Bath Abbey. The Commissioners appointed for its spoliation offered to sell the building for a small sum to the city authorities ; the offer was not accepted, and all things that could be removed—bells, lead, iron, glass—were torn from the Abbey and sold to foreign buyers. The bare walls passed by purchase into the possession of Matthew Colthurst, whose son Edmund, in 1560, presented to the city what was little better than a ruin ; and such it remained for nearly forty years.

About 1597 a move was made in the direction of restoration, in repairing and glazing the east window, and enclosing the choir so that it might be used for divine service ; but the nave and aisles were still without a roof. Bishop Montague, whose altar-tomb is a conspicuous object in the nave, added the roof and repaired the whole building between 1609 and 1616. In the meantime the Corporation, induced by greed, had granted building leases on land in the vicinity of the Abbey ; houses were built abutting the sacred edifice, so that the north aisle came to be used as a public thoroughfare. Marshal Wade, commander of the forces of the Western District at the time of the Jacobite rising early in the eighteenth century, opened out a passage through the block of houses on the north side ; and as the leases fell in, a less parsimonious Corporation pulled down buildings to provide an open space round the Abbey, besides adding spirelets to the tower turrets and nearly completing the flying buttresses.

Sir Gilbert Scott's Restoration.

In 1859, the Rev. Charles Kemble was appointed to the Rectory of Bath, and through his devotion and energy, during a period of ten years ending in 1874, and at a cost of £35,000, the Abbey was completely restored. Half the expense was borne by the rector and his family. First the fabric was made secure ; then roofs, windows and battlements were repaired ; the plaster was removed from nave, aisles and south transept, and replaced by fan tracery ; the galleries were taken down and the floor re-seated ; walls and pillars were cleaned and restored ; and the mural tablets— even at present many of them a disfigurement to the Church —were re-arranged in something approaching harmonious order—a difficult task considering how numerous the tablets are, and in many instances how uninteresting. The witty Dr. Harington, one of the most accomplished of Bath's citizens, was inspired by these tablets to the epigram :—

> "These walls adorned with monument and bust,
> Show how Bath waters serve to lay the dust."

The reredos, designed by Sir Gilbert Scott, was the gift of Mrs. Kemble after the rector's death. The font and the carved oak screen to the south of Prior Birde's Chapel were given to the Church by the congregation in token of their respect for Mr. Kemble, and their appreciation of the part he had taken in the restoration of the building.

Prior Birde's Chantry, in the southern arcade of the choir, is one of the most beautiful and interesting parts of the building. The roof is a miniature of that of the church, with the exception of the east end, where there is a demi-vault, in the centre of which are the Prior's insignia and escutcheon. The screens forming the sides of the chantry are richly adorned with delicate sculpture, and, in the spandrils of the door within, the rebus of the founder's name, a W with the figure of a bird, frequently occurs. When the monastery was suppressed the chantry was unfinished, but the original designs were completed by the liberality of the Kemble family. It has been fittingly described as " a little gem of Perpendicular memorial architecture."

The **Monuments** are so numerous as somewhat to interfere with the symmetry and noble simplicity of the church ; and, as we have said, many are of no public interest. The most conspicuous in the nave is the altar-tomb of *Bishop Montague* with his effigy, clad in episcopal robes, with a pair of Corinthian pillars at each end. Prominent in the south transept is the monument in memory of *Lady Waller*, wife of the famous Parliamentary General who was so closely connected with Somerset events of the Civil War. Sir William—the figure mutilated, not as some say by James II, for there is evidence that it was done before—is represented as mourning over his wife, and at each end is a quaintly dressed child. The inscription has a dignified opening— " To the deare memory of the right vertuous and worthy lady, Jane Lady Waller, sole daughter and heir to Sir Richard Reynell, wife of Sir William Waller, knight "—and then follows the usual poetical tribute common from that time to the end of the Georgian period.

The Corporation's gratitude for the services rendered to

the town by *Beau Nash* is shown in the monument erected at its expense to the memory of the famous M.C. ; and close to the north-east door is a marble tablet to *Quin*, the actor, a contemporary of Beau Nash. The epitaph is by David Garrick :

> "That tongue which set the table in a roar,
>   And charm'd the public ear, is heard no more;
>   Clos'd are those eyes, the harbingers of wit,
>   Which spake before the tongue what Shakespeare writ ;
>   Cold is that hand, which living was stretch'd forth,
>   At friendship's call, to succour modest worth."

Then Garrick takes the opportunity gravely to preach and moralize, thus bringing to an end the interest of the inscription.

Near the altar, on the north side of the chancel, is a beautiful monument to *Lady Miller*, whose poetical fortnightly reunions at Batheaston Villa, attended by Garrick, Anstey and others, were in refreshing contrast to the frivolities of Bath society during Beau Nash's reign. Lady Miller died in 1781. Among mural monuments of general interest are those by *Flaxman* in memory of the Hon. W. Bingham—an American Senator—and of Dr. Sibthorp, professor of botany ; and by *Chantrey* in memory of William Hoare, R.A., several of whose paintings are hung in the Guildhall, and of Admiral Bickerton.

Also recorded on these walls are the names of Dr. Broome, a translator of *Homer* ; Sarah Fielding, sister of the author of *Tom Jones* ; Dr. Harington, physician and musical composer ; Sir William Draper, the opponent of *Junius* ; Admiral Hargood, captain of the *Belleisle* at Trafalgar ; and the Rev. T. R. Malthus, famous as the writer of the *Essay on Population*.

The **Windows**, numerous, large, and many of them very beautiful, have led some admirers to call the Abbey "The Lantern of England" ; but, without going outside the county, other churches could be found equally worthy of the title. The coloured windows are modern—the whole of the windows before the Kemble restoration being of plain glass— and nearly all of them are memorials. The **East Window,** which pictures the Life of Christ, was provided by the members of the Bath Literary Club at a cost of £1,200. The great **West Window** contains a series of Old Testament subjects.

The **South Aisle Windows** have, in order, the following as subjects :—

First Window.—Christ raising the Widow's Son at Nain ;

Healing of the Centurion's Son ; Christ Blessing Little Children ; the Exhortation to " Watch and Pray " ; and the episode of the Tribute Money.

Second Window.—Moses with the Tables of the Law, and figures representing Faith, Hope, Charity and Justice.

Third Window.—Christ Healing the Sick.

Fourth Window.—The Miraculous Draught of Fishes. It is in memory of Admiral Duff, and appropriately contains texts and designs applicable to those who " go down to the sea in ships."

Fifth Window.—The Infancy of Christ.

The **North Aisle Windows,** taken in order, are as follows :—

First Window.—Hannah Praying for a Son : the Finding of Moses ; Ruth and Boaz ; Martha and Mary ; Christ and Mary ; the two Marys at the Sepulchre.

Second Window.—The Emblems of the Evangelists.

Third Window.—Scenes in the life of St. John the Baptist.

Fourth Window.—Christ's Charge to His Disciples (St. Luke xxiv. 47).

Fifth Window.—Elijah raising the Widow's Son ; the Sea giving up its Dead ; the Raising of the Widow's Son at Nain ; Samuel and Eli ; Christ as the Good Shepherd ; Timothy instructed by his Mother ; and, in the upper part of the window, figures representing Isaac, Josiah, David and Joseph.

Other Windows :—

Over West Door in North Aisle.—The Four Evangelists.

Over West Door in South Aisle.—Moses, David, Solomon and Zerubbabel, the builders of the Tabernacle and Temple.

South Transept Window.—This is known as the " Jesse Window," because it traces the descent of Christ from Jesse. It was placed as a thanksgiving for the restoration to health of the then Prince of Wales, in 1872. The lower part, surmounted by the Royal Arms and the device of the City of Bath, represents the Sickness and Recovery of Hezekiah.

The **Choir Windows :—**

Over East Door in North Choir Aisle.—Four Scenes in the Life of Christ.

Over East Door in South Choir Aisle.—The Four Evangelists.

Other North Choir Aisle Windows :—

1. Christ preaching the " Sermon on the Mount " ; and beneath it some of the Beatitudes.

2. Christ Reading the Law in the Synagogue.

3. Christ turning Water into Wine, and figures of Biblical Mothers with their children.

BATH CHURCHES

The South Choir Aisle contains a window showing, among other subjects, the Presentation in the Temple, Christ with the Doctors, and the Prophet Jeremiah.

The **Carillon**, placed in the tower at a cost of nearly £300, in 1890, plays automatically at the hours of one, five and nine a tune that varies with the day of the week, as follows : Sunday, *Easter Hymn* ; Monday, *Stella* ; Tuesday, *The Harp that once through Tara's Halls* ; Wednesday, *All Saints* ; Thursday, *Ye Banks and Braes o' Bonny Doon* ; Friday, *Come, ye Faithful* ; Saturday, *Tom Bowling.*

St. James' Church,

at the intersection of Lower Borough Walls with Southgate and Stall Street, is a stone building of Italian style, erected in 1769, and restored in 1884.

St. Michael's Church,

standing in the angle formed by Broad Street and Walcot Street, was rebuilt in 1837 in the Early English style. The well-proportioned tower, surmounted by a spire 182 feet in height, contains a peal of eight bells.

St. Swithin's Church,

the mother church of Walcot parish, is at the end of Cornwell Row, a continuation of Walcot Street. This apparently unattractive building, rebuilt in 1780, and enlarged in 1891, is, on account of its monuments, of extreme interest. Here are memorials of Madame D'Arblay—Dr. Johnson's " Little Fanny Burney "—Christopher Anstey, the witty poet of Bath ; William Hoare, the painter ; and James Hare, whose epitaph was penned by the beautiful and witty Georgiana, Duchess of Devonshire.

The remains of FRANCES BURNEY (Madame D'Arblay), author of *Evelina* and *Cecilia*, the first books written by a woman to take a place in standard literature, lie in the closed graveyard of Walcot, a little below the Church. A fitting memorial marks the spot.

St. Andrew's,

Julian Road, built in 1873 from designs by Sir Gilbert Scott, is a chapel-of-ease to St. Swithin's. The spire and west front are beautiful examples of modern application of the Early English style. The peal of eight bells and the clock, together with the alabaster reredos, pulpit and font, were given by the congregation.

HIGH STREET—MILSOM STREET—THE MUSEUM AND LIBRARY.

BATH CHURCHES

Christ Church,

in Montpelier, the eastern end of Julian Road, also belongs to Walcot parish. It was built towards the end of the eighteenth century, the chancel being added in 1866. In the tower is a fine peal of eight bells.

Close to South Parade is the Roman Catholic Church of—

St. John the Evangelist,

the most beautiful modern church in Bath, and one of the finest in the West of England. The well-proportioned interior is tastefully enriched with carvings and polished marbles. Under the slab of the marble altar is a handsome shrine containing a *corpo santo*—that of St. Justinian—and in the four panels of the reredos are carvings of scenes in the Life of St. John. At the south corner of the church is the *Chapel of St. Benedict*, at the entrance to which are statues of that saint and St. Scholastica. Within this Chapel is an alabaster reredos with events in St. Benedict's life represented in sculpture. The building throughout is rich with exquisite yet simple beauty. The English Benedictine fathers belonging to the Church live in the adjacent Priory.

St. Mary's Church, Bathwick,

was erected, at a cost of £14,000, between 1814 and 1820. The large and beautiful chancel, built from designs of the late Mr. G. E. Street, was added in 1875. In the south aisle is a window in memory of Prebendary Scarth, a writer of more than local fame as an antiquary, who was rector of Bathwick from 1841 to 1871.

PARKS AND GARDENS.

AMONG the many open spaces of Bath one of the most attractive is the—

Royal Victoria Park.

It may be reached from the centre of the city by way of Westgate Street into Monmouth Street, where the second turning to the right, Princes Street, leads along the west side of Queen Square, past the Bath and County Club, into the beautiful drive known as the **Royal Avenue**; or by keeping straight on along Monmouth Street and Monmouth Place to Upper Bristol Road, from which there is an approach to the Park near Marlborough Lane.

The first portion of Victoria Park was purchased in 1830 by voluntary subscription, and in the autumn of that year it was opened by Princess (afterwards Queen) Victoria, who was visiting Bath with her mother, the Duchess of Kent.

At the end of the Royal Avenue, approached also by the first turning to the left in Marlborough Lane, is the **Victoria Column**, erected in 1837 in celebration of Queen Victoria's coming of age; and near to it, on the triangular lawn, is the **Royal Oak**, planted by the Mayor on King Edward's wedding day, March 10, 1863. Not far from the west end of the Middle Common is an **Oak** planted in 1887 at Queen Victoria's Jubilee. On the south side of the Park is a **Lake** of three acres; and here the view is very beautiful, the ornamental water, the trees and shrubs, the flowers and grassy slopes, producing an effect of great charm. Farther on is the **Shakespeare Dell**, containing a votive altar in commemoration of the tercentenary of the poet's birth. Hard by, the pedestal adorned with ivy and other creeping plants, is a colossal head of *Jupiter*, fashioned out of a single block of Bath stone by John Osborne, a self-taught native artist.

Not only is the Victoria Park a great attraction, but it has an educational value, for the trees and plants, representative of almost every species in Britain, are labelled both with their botanical and their English names.

The **Botanical Gardens,** at the north-west corner of the Park, close to the Park Lane entrance, contain the fine collection of herbaceous plants gathered by the late Mr. C. Broome, and presented by his executors. The value of the Gardens has been increased by subsequent gifts ; and with the rockeries and lawns, and the varied beauty of trees and shrubs, they form a charming resort for the general visitor as well as a school of botany for the scientific.

Henrietta Park,

on the north of Great Pulteney Street, is an area of 7 acres given to the city in 1895 by Captain Forester, who inherited the Bathwick estates from the Duke of Cleveland. Formerly a field, the place was transformed into an attractive park by the skill and artistic taste of the late Mr. J. W. Morris.

Behind Pulteney Street, on the opposite side, is—

The Recreation Ground,

the scene of most of the important local athletic events. These extensive and well-kept grounds, the rendezvous of every kind of outdoor sport, are charmingly situated in the heart of the City, and command delightful views of the surrounding hills. The **Somerset County Cricket Club** play first-class matches every season on the ground in connection with the County Championship, and these occasions are attended with various social functions. Athletic, cycling, hockey, tennis and croquet tournaments are also arranged, the athletic meeting being of much importance. In the winter the *Bath Football Club* (Rugby) fight out their battles with strong West of England and Welsh teams.

Great Pulteney Street terminates at the entrance to—

Sydney Gardens,

beautifully laid out with lawns and tree-shaded walks. This pleasantly wooded retreat, now the property of the Corporation, was formerly managed by the Floral Fête and Band Committee, who rendered splendid service to the City by their successful and voluntary efforts to add to its amusements. A recent addition to the Gardens is a replica, on a slightly reduced scale, of the portico of the Roman Temple

erected to the worship of Sul Minerva. The
Floral Fêtes, usually held in July and August, when the
illuminated gardens make a singularly pretty scene, attract
not only residents in Bath, but visitors from miles around ;
and equally popular is the Children's Carnival. The **Band,**
under the control of the Corporation, plays every week-day
afternoon and evening during the summer either in the
Gardens, or on the Band Lawn in Victoria Park, or in the—

Institution Gardens

on the North Parade, where the waters may be sipped from
the **Fountain** in the Colonnade, to the accompaniment of
music, under pleasant open-air conditions.

It would be difficult to find more beautifully situated
grounds. The Avon, broad and placid, flows along one side.
Beyond a deep splashing weir—a mass of snow-white foam
glistening in the sunshine—is Pulteney Bridge, designed by
Robert Adam in 1771. Three stone arches span the river,
and over these are shops and houses. Across the Avon the
Recreation Ground and County Cricket Field stretch away
to the tree-covered slopes of Hampton Down. Higher up
on the Down are the Bath Golf Links ; and the curious Sham
Castle, erected by Ralph Allen " to improve the prospect "
from his town house, is a conspicuous feature.

ROYAL VICTORIA PARK.

FAMOUS BATH RESIDENTS.

ONE of the most interesting features in the history of Bath is its association, principally during the seventeenth and eighteenth centuries, with many of the most distinguished representatives of religion, politics, literature, science and art. The Corporation have affixed a number of **Mural Tablets** upon the houses where people of renown have resided. The tablets are frequently receiving additions, and soon the whole history of Bath during two centuries will be written upon its walls.

Within a distance of less than 200 yards from the Abbey Churchyard are the following historical houses :—

No. 14, Abbey Churchyard.—*Marshal Wade*, the early friend of Ralph Allen, and M.P. for Bath, lived here from 1722–41.

Town House, back of North Street.—This is in a *cul-de-sac* opening out of the west end of North Parade. Town house of *Ralph Allen* about 1720.

The **Museum**, Royal Literary and Scientific Institution.— A tablet records that the three poets, *Thomas Moore, George Crabbe*, and *W. Lisle Bowles*, were present at the banquet when the building was opened on January 19, 1825.

Bowles, now almost forgotten as a poet, was the pioneer of a school of poetry that became very popular in his day and the merits of which were acknowledged and imitated by Wordsworth and Coleridge. Byron, who in his *English Bards and Scotch Reviewers* lashed with his wit Scott and Southey, Wordsworth and Coleridge, did not spare Bowles, of whom he said " All love thy strain, but children like it best." In speaking of Bowles' *Sonnets* he, however, could address the author as " Harmonious Bowles," and " Delightful Bowles," and pay him the tribute, " Stick to thy sonnets, man ! At least they sell." It is chiefly by these sonnets that Bowles keeps a place in literature.

No. 4, North Parade.—*John Wilkes*, the champion of the freedom of the Press, imprisoned, fined and outlawed for attacking the Government in his newspaper, *The North Briton*, in the reign of George III, was a frequent visitor here between 1760 and 1770.

FAMOUS RESIDENTS

No. 9, North Parade.—*William Wordsworth* lodged in this house during 1841.

No. 10, North Parade.—The *Duke of York*, brother of George III, lived here in 1761.

No. 11, North Parade.—Associated with *Oliver Goldsmith* in 1771, and with *Edmund Burke* in 1797.

No. 6, South Parade.—*Sir Walter Scott* lived here for a short time when a child, with his uncle.

No. 5, Pierrepont Street (the street connecting North and South Parades on the west).—*Elizabeth Anna Linley*, the " Maid of Bath," who became the wife of Richard Brinsley Sheridan, was born here in 1751.

Nos. 3a and 4, Pierrepont Street (formerly one house).— The residence of *Lord Chesterfield*, at intervals between 1738 and 1771. Here he wrote many of the famous *Letters* to his son. *Quin*, the famous actor, died at this house in 1766.

No. 2, Pierrepont Street.—*Lord Nelson* stayed here during 1780–81, after his return from a voyage to the Polar Seas with Captain Phipps' expedition.

No. 7, Terrace Walk.—*Sheridan* is believed to have written *The Rivals* here.

Westward from the Abbey.

No. 39, Westgate Street, the residence in 1772 of *Josiah Wedgwood*, the famous potter.

From Westgate Street take first turning on left into St. Michael's Lane and first on right into Westgate Buildings.

Chapel Court, Westgate Buildings.—*Horace Walpole* resided here in 1765.

Hetling House, Nowhere Lane, off Westgate Buildings.— *Princess Amelia* stayed here for a short time. *Alexander Pope* also visited the house.

From Westgate enter Kingsmead Square.

Londonderry House, Kingsmead Square.—At this house, on west side of Square, *Bishop Butler*, of *Analogy* fame, died in 1752 ; *Sheridan* also lived here.

At the west end of Kingsmead Street is Charles Street. Turn to left, and on opposite side of road is—

No. 22, Charles Street, where *Gibbon*, the author of *The Decline and Fall of the Roman Empire*, was a frequent visitor to his stepmother.

Westward of Charles Street is—

FAMOUS RESIDENTS

No. 19, New King Street, the house where *Herschel* made his discovery of the planet Uranus in 1781.

At top of New King Street turn to left in Stanhope Street, which leads to—

No. 15, Norfolk Buildings, where *Miss Muloch* (Mrs. Craik), the author of *John Halifax, Gentleman,* lived in 1874.

South of the Midland Railway Station is—

No. 25, Green Park, where *Sir William P. Napier,* in 1841-2, wrote his *History of the Peninsular War.*

From Pulteney Bridge to Sydney Gardens.

Cross the Bridge, and at the end of Argyle Street, on the right, is—

No. 8, Argyle Street, the residence of *Lord St. Vincent.*

On the right, in Argyle Street, is the—

Congregational Chapel.—A tablet in front of the building commemorates the ministry there for sixty-two years (1791–1853) of the *Rev. William Jay,* the finest pulpit orator of his time. He was held in high esteem by all denominations.

No. 15, Johnston Street, the house where *William Pitt* lived when he visited Bath in 1802.

Returning to Laura Place and continuing in the direction of Sydney Gardens, the visitor will pass on the right—

No. 59, Great Pulteney Street, where *Bishop Thirlwall,* the historian, died in 1874.

Bearing to the left, there will be seen—

No. 103, Sydney Place, the residence in 1817 of the *Duke of Clarence,* afterwards William IV ; and—

No. 93, Sydney Place, where, in the same year, *Queen Charlotte* lived.

Opposite the house occupied by the Duke of Clarence is a turning leading to the—

Sydney Gardens Hotel, the hostelry at which *Prince Napoleon,* afterwards the Emperor Louis Napoleon, stayed during his visit to Bath in 1846.

By keeping straight on, the north end of Sydney Place is reached, and on the opposite side is—

No. 4, Sydney Place, the residence in 1801-5 of *Jane Austen,* whose descriptions of Bath life adorn the pages of several of her novels.

Reached to the left out of the north end of Sydney Gardens is—

FAMOUS RESIDENTS

No. 16, Bathwick Street, associated with *Thomas Barker,* the painter of *The Woodman.* He twice painted this picture ; the earlier work, done in his youth, is to be seen in the Victoria Art Gallery.

By returning along the right of Great Pulteney Street there will be seen the following interesting houses :—

No. 36, Great Pulteney Street, where *William Wilberforce* lived for a short time in 1802: and **No. 2,** in the same street, at which, when it was Stead's Hotel, *Edward Bulwer* (*Lord*) *Lytton* stayed at various times between 1867 and 1872.

Keep to the right round the north side of Laura Place, and there will be reached—

No. 37, Henrietta Street, from 1836–8 the residence of *Sir Charles J. Napier.* At No. 9, in the same street, he lived for a short time in apartments.

From Westgate Street to the Circus.

The turning to the right at the west end of Westgate Street leads to—

Saw Close, in which is the *Garrick's Head,* the residence of *Beau Nash.* He died in the adjoining house.

Reached by a turning on the right is—

No. 5, Trim Street, from which *General Wolfe* started, in 1759, on the expedition which ended in his death in the hour of victory at Quebec.

From Wolfe's house return in the direction of Saw Close, and turn to the right along Barton Street into Gay Street.

No. 24, Queen Square (on the north side, reached by a turning to the left out of Gay Street).—Here died, in 1754, the celebrated architect, *John Wood, senior,* whose designs for the building of the Circus did much to add to the attractions of Bath as a residential resort.

No. 41, Gay Street (corner of King Street).—The residence of *John Wood, junior,* who designed the Royal Crescent. Here Fanny Burney lived.

On the opposite side of the road is—

No. 8, Gay Street, the home from 1781–1821 of *Mrs. Piozzi* (formerly *Mrs. Thrale,* a friend of Dr. Johnson).

No. 15, Gay Street.—Here lived, from 1780–1810, *Rauzzini,* a celebrated Bath musician. David Garrick and Incledon frequently visited him at this house. At the top of Gay Street is—

FAMOUS RESIDENTS

The Circus,

the pioneer structure in the architectural beauty of Bath. Almost every other house is famous as the abode of some celebrated visitor or resident. In the following list we start from the turning to the left out of Gay Street.

No. 4.—*Sir Roderick Murchison* resided here for a time when making observations on the geology of the neighbourhood.

No. 5.—The home for a brief period of *W. M. Thackeray.*

Nos. 7 and 8.—*William Pitt, Earl of Chatham,* lived here during 1755–63.

No. 9.—*Lord Leighton's* residence in 1866.

No. 13.—*Dr. Livingstone* stayed here for a short time, in 1864, while on a brief visit to England after his survey of the Zambesi River.

No. 14.—*Lord Clive's* residence during the months of ill-health and depression of spirits that preceded his death in 1774.

No. 22.—A tablet records that here lived, in 1770, *Major André,* Adjutant-General in the British Army during the war that led to the independence of the United States ; but the fact is somewhat doubtful, because in Major André's time this part of the Circus was not in a habitable condition. Some time afterwards, however, the house was the temporary residence of some members of his family.

No. 24.—*Thomas Gainsborough* resided here in 1770, when at the height of his fame as a portrait painter.

The first turning to the left from the Gay Street entrance to the Circus is Brock Street, leading into the most striking example of the domestic architecture of Bath—

The Royal Crescent.

No. 5.—Here lived *Christopher Anstey,* the author of the *New Bath Guide,* a volume of verse the pointed and original humour of which was greatly admired at the time, and is still read with interest.

No. 9.—*Edward Bulwer (Lord) Lytton* resided here in 1866.

No. 17.—*Sir Isaac Pitman,* for sixty years resident in Bath, the inventor of the most widely-used system of shorthand, died here, January, 1897, in his eighty-fifth year.

FAMOUS RESIDENTS

North of Royal Crescent.

At the Brock Street end of the Royal Crescent turn north-wards along Upper Church Street, and at the second turning to the right will be seen—

No. 3, Rivers Street, on the left, the home, in 1852, of *Walter Savage Landor*, who lived in Bath from 1837 to 1857, when he left England for ever after being mulcted in £1,000 damages for libelling a Bath lady.

Return to Upper Church Street, and nearly opposite Rivers Street is Crescent Lane, out of which on the right St. James' Street leads into—

St. James' Square, Nos. 1 and 35 of which were also residences of *Landor*. At No. 35 *Dickens* stayed.

The north-west corner of this Square is the approach to—

No. 21, Park Street, the residence from 1852–60 of the eloquent *Dr. Magee*, afterwards Archbishop of York.

The visitor should now retrace his steps, and the first turning to the right, Cavendish Place, leads to Summerhill Road, out of which the first on the right is a road leading to—

Summerhill Park, the birthplace, in 1790, of *Sir William Parry*, the Arctic explorer.

From Summerhill Road, east end, it is a direct walk along Lansdown Place West to—

Beckford House, Lansdown Crescent, the home, from 1822 to his death in 1844, of *William Beckford*, famous for his vast wealth, his eccentricities, and his great literary talents.

Beckford was born in 1761, the son of a London alderman ; and in his tenth year, at his father's death, Lord Chatham undertook the guidance of his education. He was not twenty years of age when his first book was published, *Biographical Memoirs of Extra-ordinary Painters*, a satire in which he ridiculed English artists of his own time. In 1796 he began the building of the magnificent mansion of Fonthill, in Wiltshire, which he furnished with a beauty and luxury that were the wonder of visitors. Here he lived until 1822, when, owing to the loss of two large estates successfully claimed in Chancery by other owners, he disposed of Fonthill, the house, furniture and estates realizing £330,000. For the rest of his days he lived at Beckford House, Lansdown Crescent. His literary fame depends on *Vathek*, an eastern tale written in French at a single sitting extending, it is said, over three days and two nights. The tale, which is still read, made a great impression upon Lord Byron, who wrote concerning it : " For beauty of description and power of imagination, this most eastern and sublime tale far surpasses all European imitation."

QUEEN SQUARE.

PULTENEY BRIDGE AND WEIRS.

FAMOUS RESIDENTS

From Milsom Street to the Assembly Rooms.

No. 38, Milsom Street.—*Field-Marshal Sir Robert Rich* died here, 1768.

No. 4, Edgar Buildings (top of Milsom Street).—Here lived, in 1790, the year before her death, the **Countess of Huntingdon**, who, on her adoption of Methodism, appointed George Whitefield as her chaplain. At Whitefield's death his followers became known as *Lady Huntingdon's Connexion*.

York House Hotel, Prince's Buildings (a continuation eastward of Edgar Buildings).—Here *Queen Victoria* stayed when, as Princess Victoria, she visited Bath with her mother in 1830. A tablet marks the room she occupied.

Running north from this thoroughfare is Bartlett Street, at the top of which a turning to the right leads to—

No. 2, Alfred Street, the residence (1785–8) of *Sir Thomas Lawrence* when, in his youth, he came to study portrait painting in Bath.

Parallel on the north with Alfred Street is Bennet Street, reached either by Belmont or Saville Row. To the right, and on the same side as Saville Row, is—

No. 2, Bennet Street, where the *father and the wife of Lord Nelson* lived in 1802. At—

No. 19, Bennet Street, the *Rev. Legh Richmond*, author of *The Dairyman's Daughter*, etc., resided from 1786–94.

Widcombe Lodge.—*Fielding* and his sister Sarah frequently stayed at this house as the guests of Philip Bennet, lord of the Manor of Widcombe.

"Here," says Mr. Peach in his *Bath : Old and New,* "portions at least of *Tom Jones* were written in the room invariably assigned to him on those occasions—namely, the room with the oval window in the centre of the pediment in the south front."

Referring to Fielding's sister, Mr. Peach remarks—"She was richly endowed with intellectual gifts, and the moral graces of her character and the charms of her conversation made her a special favourite with Ralph Allen and the circle at Prior Park."

In the second house of a row of buildings known as **Fielding's Terrace,** in Twerton, *Henry Fielding* wrote several chapters of *Tom Jones.*

Prior Park is associated with many illustrious names.

WALKS AROUND BATH.

I. TO BEECHEN CLIFF.

THE most prominent natural object seen from Bath is
Beechen Cliff, which returns the compliment by affording the best view that can be had of the city from any position.

Leaving the Abbey by Stall Street, continue along Southgate Street, cross the Old Bridge (a fourteenth-century
structure) and pass beneath a railway arch ; then we shall
have on our right Warwick Place, the lower end of Wells
Road ; on our left, Claverton Street, leading to the thoroughfare called Lyncombe Hill ; and in front, stretching in a
south-westerly direction, the steep road known as Holloway.
Those who prefer a gentler, if longer ascent, will follow the
Wells Road which, after a winding course, joins Holloway
at the *Bear Inn*.

When half-way up Holloway we come to the small **Chapel
of St. Mary Magdalen**, erected by John Cantlow, Prior of
Bath, on the site of a much older building. Upwards we
go until within a few yards of the *Bear Inn*, where, on the
opposite side of the road to the chapel, we follow the winding
lane known as Prospect Place. A short alley on the left
leads to—

Beechen Cliff,

a precipitous mass, 400 feet high. Beneath, as in a map,
the city is spread. Below is the winding Avon, and towering
high above the surrounding buildings is the stately Abbey.
In front of it is St. James' Church ; at the back is St. Michael's
Church. Opposite us, and behind the city, is Lansdown
Hill, up whose slopes creep the houses of Lansdown, Camden
and Cavendish Crescents. West of Lansdown, crowned by
a clump of trees, is Kelston Round Hill, and farther to the
west, but nearer to our standpoint, is Englishcombe Barrow.
To the north-west is plainly seen the Royal Crescent with
the adjacent Victoria Park. Turning to the east we see
Hampton Down, with the castellated make-believe Sham

Castle; and the more distant height to the north-east is Solsbury Hill, the deeply interesting connection of which with prehistoric Bath we have referred to in the section devoted to the history of the city.

The return to Bath may be made by turning left to the zig-zag steps leading to the terrace, or by turning to the right for Lyncombe Hill. Those who wish for a longer walk can return by the way they came—the winding lane to Holloway—and on to the *Bear Inn*. About a quarter of a mile beyond two roads meet, Wells Road on the left, and Old Wells Road on the right. Following the latter, we cross a tunnel on the Somerset and Dorset Railway, and at the next road junction bear to right along Englishcombe Lane. The places of interest to which this lane leads are **Berewyke Camp,** opposite Crescent Cottage, a portion of the historic Wansdyke, **Odd Down** and **Englishcombe.**

From Beechen Cliff to Englishcombe and back to Bath is a walk of about four miles.

II. TO TWERTON AND KELSTON.

The way lies along Southgate Street, across the Old Bridge, and then by Lower Bristol Road to the Midland Railway Bridge, at a distance of about three-quarters of a mile from our starting point. On the left is the **Cemetery** for the united parishes of Lyncombe, Widcombe and St. James'. **Twerton** and some of the places of interest approached from it, such as Newton St. Loe and Corston, are referred to in our description of the tramcar route to that industrial suburb.

By a road running northward from Corston we reach, after ten minutes' walk, the highway. A turning to the left leads us parallel with the railway; and just beyond the station on the right we turn along a cross road to **Saltford,** near the church being the ancient mansion of the Rodneys. Crossing the river by the ferry, we go over the fields to—

Kelston,

the manorial rights of which belonged to Shaftesbury Abbey before the Dissolution of the Monasteries. It afterwards passed into the possession of a courtier, John Harington, the father of Sir John Harington, the witty and learned knight, godson of Queen Elizabeth, and ever a good friend to Bath. In the summer of 1591 the Queen visited Sir John, and some of the trees that she planted still remain, but not the original mansion. It was damaged during the Civil War, and eventually pulled down. The present house, on the brow of a hill overlooking the river, and occupying the site of the old summer-house, was built in 1760 by Wood, the architect, for Sir Cæsar Hawkins, the King's physician.

Kelston Church, rebuilt in 1860, contains portions of the earlier structure of Henry II's time, an Elizabethan font, and two piscinæ. There are also a few relics of the original Saxon church.

From Kelston we return to Bath, about 3 miles distant, by the Upper Bristol Road, which is continued to Bath by way of Monmouth Street and Westgate Street.

III. TO WESTON, PROSPECT STILE AND SWAINSWICK.

From the Abbey, keep along High Street and Broad Street to the top of Belmont, where turn to left along Montpelier, passing **Christ Church** on the right. Montpelier runs into Julian Road, and this again into Weston Road, leading to **Weston,** less than 2 miles to the north-west of the city. The village and the neighbouring **Prospect Stile,** on Stoke Brow, are described in the section devoted to the tramcar route to Weston. About a mile from the stile, approached by a road running eastward, is **Upper Langridge,** and ten minutes' walk beyond is **Langridge,** on the eastern ridge of Lansdown Hill, and commanding wide and varied views. Langridge Church contains an inner Norman doorway and a chancel arch, only 7 feet wide, belonging to the same period. The tower and font are Early English.

Half a mile from Langridge we cross the Avon, turn to the right, and a quarter of an hour's walk brings us to—

Upper Swainswick.

Antiquaries differ as to this name. Some say it is a corruption of Swineswick, and that here Bladud served as a swineherd; others think it to be a combination of *Swain*, the name of a Saxon lord, and *wick*, a village; while again a third theory connects it with the Danish King Sweyn. Near the **Church,** a mixture of architectural periods from the Norman to the Perpendicular, is the **Manor House,** now a farmhouse. Overlooking the village is **Solsbury Hill,** a stiff climb, but worth the trouble for the fine views to be had from the summit. At the foot of the hill are reservoirs that supply Bath with water. Along Gloucester Road it is a five minutes' walk to London Road, the main thoroughfare into Bath.

IV. TO CHARLCOMBE, BECKFORD'S TOWER AND GRENVILLE'S MONUMENT.

Straight on by way of High Street, Broad Street and Belmont into Lansdown Road. At the corner by St. Stephen's Church turn to the right along Richmond Road for three-quarters of a mile to—

Charlcombe,

a quaint and romantic village in a secluded vale. The **Church,** overshadowed by a venerable yew, is interesting as the scene of the marriage of Henry Fielding, the novelist, to Charlotte Craddock, on November 28, 1734. Here his sister, Sarah Fielding, was buried on April 14, 1768. The building has an inner Norman arch and a walled-up doorway of the same period on the north side.

Returning along Richmond Road, we reach by a narrow lane on the right, opposite Charlcombe Manor, Lansdown Road, and there turn to the right for—

Beckford's Tower,

less than a mile distant. The Tower, situated on the summit of **Lansdown,** 813 feet above sea-level, is named after its builder, the eccentric Mr. Beckford, of Fonthill Abbey.

A circular staircase leads to the top, from which is to be had the finest view in the neighbourhood of Bath. Indeed, it was with an appreciation of the prospect afforded that it was erected ; for Beckford, in building the Tower and choosing it as a place for retirement, wished to be within daily sight of his Wiltshire mansion at Fonthill, 26 miles away.

Close to the fourth milestone from Bath is—

Grenville's Monument,

an obelisk in memory of Sir Bevil Grenville, one of the commanders in the Royalist force in the **Battle of Lansdown** (July 5, 1643). After a stubborn encounter lasting for hours, the Parliamentary Army, led by Sir William Waller, retired, and the Royalists claimed the victory. But the triumph was dearly purchased in the death of Sir Bevil, who fell when opposing a cavalry charge. The monument was erected to his memory in 1720 by a kinsman, Lord Lansdown. On one of the tablets is an allusion to Sir Bevil's famous ancestor, Sir Richard Grenville, the subject of Tennyson's spirited ballad, *The Revenge*.

> " Thus slain thy valiant ancestor did lie,
> When his one bark a navy did defy,
> When now encompass'd round he victor stood,
> And bath'd his pinnace in his conquering blood,
> Till all his purple current dry'd and spent,
> He fell, and made the waves his monument.
> Where shall the next fam'd *Grenville's* ashes stand ?
> The grandsire fills the seas, and thou the land."

On another tablet is a quotation from the account of the Battle of Lansdown given by Lord Clarendon in his *History of the Rebellion* :—

" In this battle, on the King's part, were more officers and gentlemen of quality slain than private men ; but that which would have clouded any victory, and made the loss of others less spoken of, was the death of Sir Bevil Grenville: he was indeed an excellent person, whose activity, interest and reputation was the foundation of what had been done in Cornwall, and his temper and affection so public, that no accident which happened could make any impression in him ; and his example kept others from taking anything ill, or at least seeming to do so : in a word, a brighter courage and a gentler disposition was never married together, to make the most cheerful and innocent conversation."

On Lansdown are many ancient earthworks, the road close to the monument passing through a Roman Camp. The house on the right, a little below the monument, stands on the site of the fortified post scaled by Sir Bevil's troops a few minutes before the final charge.

Wick.

Two miles northward is the village of Wick, situated in a rocky romantic valley, formed by cleavage in the mass of limestone. Prettily wooded, with cliffs on both sides rising to the height of 200 feet, and through it a brook flowing, the valley is rich in romantic charm. Its geology, botany and scenery are unlike those of other places within walking distance of Bath. Near the village is a cromlech. Those who like a change on the journey home may take train from *Warmley Station*, 3 miles from Wick.

BATHAMPTON

V. TO BATHAMPTON, BATHEASTON AND ST. CATHERINE.

Cross Pulteney Bridge, the houses on both sides of which hide the river from view, and by way of Argyle Street and Laura Place enter Great Pulteney Street, one of the finest thoroughfares in Bath. The *Fountain* in the middle of Laura Place was erected in commemoration of the centenary meeting of the Bath and West of England Society's Show, held at Bath in 1877. Great Pulteney Street terminates at the entrance to Sydney Gardens. On the right, at the end of Pulteney Street, is Darlington Street, containing **St. Mary's Church,** noted for the beauty of its structure and its musical services. Our way to Bathampton, 2 miles from Bath, is to the left of Sydney Gardens, along Sydney Place. Passing on the left Bathwick Street, where is situated **St. John's Church,** a graceful building with choir and organ exceptionally good, we bear to the right along the Gardens and, instead of turning under the railway arch, keep straight on by the *Kennet and Avon Canal* to the pretty village of **Bathampton.** The Church is a Perpendicular structure, with traces of Early English in the chancel. In the churchyard is the grave of John Baptiste, Viscount du Barré, who was killed in a duel with Colonel Rice, on Claverton Down, in 1778. Rice and his seconds were tried for murder at Taunton, but acquitted. We reach **Batheaston** and St. Catherine by crossing the river.

VI. TO CLAVERTON AND SHAM CASTLE.

There are several routes to Claverton, the most pleasant being by way of Sydney Gardens, as shown in Walk V, and turning to right out of the Bathampton Road, about a mile beyond the entrance to the Gardens. A quarter of a mile farther brings us to **Hampton Rocks,** a landslip noted for the fine views to be obtained over the neighbouring country. North-west of the rocks is the site of the British city, **Caer Badon,** where vestiges of ancient works will be recognized by antiquaries. Close by is a portion of the **Wansdyke.**
Continuing along the road past some woodlands we have near to us, on the left, canal, railway, and the Avon. After a walk of 3 miles from Sidney Gardens we reach **Claverton**, prettily situated in the winding valley of the Avon.

A road running almost due west from the village leads

to **Bathwick Hill.** In the charmingly situated little cemetery of **Bathwick** is the grave of *W. Clark Russell* (d. 1911), the famous writer of sea stories. Not far away is **Sham Castle.**

From Bathwick Hill we enter George Street, which takes us, by way of Raby Place and Darlington Street, to the Sydney Gardens entrance.

VII. TO PRIOR PARK AND COMBE DOWN.

Cross the Old Bridge, and turn to left along Claverton Street, which leads into Widcombe Parade, at the end of which bear to the right along Prior Park Road ; then, skirting the Abbey Cemetery and the Roman Catholic Cemetery on the left, we enter the carriage road along **Prior Park.** A hundred feet above the mansion is **Combe Down.** The district is described on pp. 100–101.

A gate leads out of the road beyond Combe Down to Monument Field, and, crossing this, with the monument on the right and the Park on the left, we reach **Widcombe Old Church,** built by Prior Birde, in 1500, on the site of an earlier structure. The churchyard was a favourite spot with Walter Savage Landor, who purchased here a plot for his own resting-place ; but, dying at Florence, he was buried there. Near the Church is **Widcombe House,** described as " second only to Prior Park in architectural dignity and beauty of situation." The road is direct by way of Cambridge Place into Claverton Street.

VIII. TO MIDFORD, WELLOW AND COMBE HAY.

This is a pleasant excursion, but as it necessitates a walk of 11 miles, many will prefer the assistance of the Midland Railway to Midford, or farther on to Wellow. The walking route is by way of Stall Street, Southgate Street, over the Old Bridge and up Holloway to the *Bear Inn,* on the Wells road ; a quarter of a mile beyond turn to the left, and again to the left, near the railway, along Entry Hill. At *Cross Keys Inn,* a little more than a mile from the railway, the road on the left leads near to **Midford Castle,** a picturesque modern residence, and on to pleasantly situated—

Midford,

a mile from the inn, and 3 miles from Bath. Here lived and worked William Smith, the " Father of English Geology," who found profitable occupation in studying the beds between the Oolitic series of rocks and the Upper Lias. The long tunnel between Bath and Midford was cut through these "passage beds," as they are called, an interesting section being exposed to view at the village end of the tunnel approach.

Continuing our walk westward for nearly a mile along a road almost parallel with the Canal, we come to the meeting of four roads, the one on the left leading us across the Canal and a tributary of the Avon. A mile and a half beyond that is—

Wellow,

with a station on the Somerset and Dorset Railway, 6 miles from Bath. The **Church,** rebuilt in 1372 by Sir Walter Hungerford, and completed in Henry VII's time, was restored in 1845, and a new chancel added in 1890 as a memorial of the late vicar. The most interesting features are the Hungerford, or Lady Chapel, with the tomb of Sir Walter Hungerford, a prominent personage in West of England history; the Early English font and richly carved roof; and the effigy of an ecclesiastic, discovered during the restoration of the church, and placed in a recess on the north side of the chancel. On the forehead is an incised Maltese cross. Near the churchyard is the manor-house of the Hungerfords, now used as a farmhouse.

In a field called *Wellow Hayes*, less than a mile from the village, Roman pavements and coins have been found.

About 1½ miles north-west of Wellow is the secluded village of—

Combe Hay,

the manorial rights of which were owned by Odo, Bishop of Bayeux, half-brother of the Conqueror. He was succeeded by the Harveys, who held the manor until the reign of Edward I; and it is curious that the village is sometimes locally called Harvey. The **Church,** a modern structure with a fifteenth-century tower, contains a tablet in memory of Carrington, author of *Dartmoor* and other poems widely read at the time. He died at Bath in 1830, and in the churchyard of Combe Hay his grave is marked by a Gothic tomb.

From the village we return by way of Fortnight Hill to *Burnt House Inn*, about a mile away, and keeping to the right along the Wells road repass the *Bear Inn.*

ELECTRIC TRAM ROUTES.

THE country around Bath teems with charm and interest; but the hilly nature of the surroundings makes some of the walks, especially in summer, laborious to all but the young and active; and even when a vehicle is engaged the stiff ascents necessitate slow driving, too tedious to be exhilarating. Places like Lansdown and Combe Down would be practically inaccessible to the majority of visitors without the aid of the electric tram or motor 'bus; and that these airy heights are brought within easy reach from Bath is a distinct addition to the many attractions of the city.

I. THE GUILDHALL TO BATHFORD.

Fares.—Guildhall (or Old Bridge) to Lambridge, 1d. Lambridge to Batheaston (Post Office), 1d. Batheaston to Bathford, 1d. Bath to Bathford, 3d.

The cars to Bathford run by way of Broad Street and the Paragon, along the London Road to Lambridge. Here the town ends and the country begins. Looking to the right as the car moves on from Lambridge, the passenger will have a fine view of the hills encircling Bath on the south and east.

Before entering Batheaston there will be seen **Bathampton Weirs,** over which a road runs to Bathampton. The end of the 2d. stage is the post office at—

Batheaston.

This populous village, 2½ miles from Bath, has a delightful situation. The **Church,** originally a thirteenth-century structure, was rebuilt and enlarged in 1833, the materials of the Decorated south wall and porch of the old church being replaced in the present south aisle and porch. The nave and the tower are Perpendicular work, and one of the tower buttresses possesses a stair turret crowned by a beautiful pinnacle. The organ chamber was erected by Captain Struan Robertson, brother of the celebrated Brighton preacher in memory of his father, Captain F. Robertson, and is in harmony with the architecture of the chancel.

Not far from the church is a house, distinguished by a stone eagle, which was the country residence of John Wood, to whom Bath owes so much of its architectural glory. The literary associations connected with **Batheaston Villa**, which the trams pass on the left, have already been described.

The Batheaston post-office is the stopping-place for those who wish to visit—

St. Catherine,

a hamlet situated in a delightful vale, about 1½ miles north of Batheaston. The **Church,** which contains a Norman font of Caen stone, dates from the end of the fifteenth century. The east window is a memorial of Prior Cantlow, the founder of the present structure.

In the hamlet is the picturesque Elizabethan manor-house known as **St. Catherine's Court.** The house formerly belonged to Bath Abbey, whose dignitaries used to seek rest here amid the surrounding vineyards and gardens.

Returning to the tramway at Batheaston, we continue the route along the river-side to—

Bathford,

a village prettily situated on a steep declivity of **Farleigh Down**, at the foot of which a small stream called *Box Brook* enters the Avon. In the parish stands **Shockerwick House,** built in 1750 from designs by John Wood, senior, and improved and enlarged during the last few years. Queen Victoria, when visiting Bath as Princess Victoria, was taken by her mother to view the pictures at Shockerwick. Fine views of the surrounding country are to be had from the grounds and vicinity. **Bathford Church** contains a Norman doorway and font, with an Early English archway in the porch.

WALKS FROM BATHFORD.

There are several places of interest within walking distance of Bathford. By a road running south-eastward it is 1½ miles to—

Monkton Farleigh,

a village situated on a hill on the borders of Somerset and Wiltshire. The **Manor House,** once the property of the Duke of Somerset, stands upon the site of an old Cluniac convent, parts of which are incorporated with the present building. A short distance north-west of the house is the little Gothic structure sheltering what is known as the *Monk's Conduit*, which formed the water supply for the old convent. The **Church** (St. Peter's) is in the Norman and Early English styles.

A good road leads from Monkton Farleigh in 2 miles to—

South Wraxall.

The **Manor House** is a very interesting example of mediæval domestic architecture. Leland thus writes of the origin of the family whose descendants have owned the house in unbroken succession since its erection : " One Long Thomas, a stoute felaw, was sette up by one of the old Lordes Hungerfordes, and after by cause this Thomas was called Long Thomas, Long was usurped as the name of the family." The present representative of the family is the Right Hon. W. H. Long, M.P. The entrance gateway with the oriel window above is the oldest part. The dining room is Elizabethan, and the drawing-room Jacobean. South Wraxall Manor House is one of the places said to be the first in England in which tobacco was smoked ; and the guest chamber is pointed out as the room in which Sir Walter Raleigh lighted his silver pipe in company with his host, Sir Walter Long. The Manor House was for a brief period used as a school by Dr. Knight, of *She Wore a Wreath of Roses* fame.

The **Church** is a Perpendicular structure, restored in 1882.

Two miles to the south-east is—

Great Chalfield,

also with a fine **Manor House**, a fifteenth-century erection. Pugin, in his *Examples of Gothic Architecture* (vol. iii.), says : " The north front is nearly perfect, with its porch and groined roof, the hall in its centre flanked by a gabled building at each end, each with an oriel. The whole front is one of the finest and most elaborate that we have." The barns and other farm buildings were added in Elizabeth's reign.

The ancient **Church** has many features of interest to the antiquary.

A very pretty walk may be taken from the Bathford tram terminus to **Brown's Folly**, a tower that is a conspicuous landmark for many miles round. It was built by Mr. Wade

Brown as an observatory, and its prominence always arouses the curiosity of strangers.

II. THE GUILDHALL TO COMBE DOWN.

Fares.—Guildhall to *Devonshire Arms*, 1d. *Devonshire Arms* to Glasshouse Farm, 1d. Glasshouse Farm to Combe Down, 1d. All the way, 3d.;

The cars to Combe Down run down Southgate Street and over the Old Bridge. They then ascend for nearly two miles in a gradient which is sometimes one in ten. The *Devonshire Arms*, the end of the 1d. stage, is nearly a mile and a half from the city. Still ascending, the route runs over the tunnel of the Somerset and Dorset Railway ; and from the top of the cars a fine view may be had of the railway threading the beautiful valley before it enters the Combe Down tunnel. The ride is still upwards to the *Union*, where, at the road junction on the Bath side of the building, many passengers descend to explore the places of interest in the neighbourhood.

Less than a quarter of a mile along the road branching from the tram route, is a turning to the right leading to **Odd Down**, where another turning to the right, at the Congregational Chapel, leads to Crescent Cottages, a few hundred yards away. Opposite is **Berewyke Camp,** a British fort with earth mounds and a ditch.

WALKS FROM ODD DOWN.

If the visitor fond of walking will retrace his steps to Odd Down, and then turn to the right, he will reach, about a mile away, **High Barrow Hill,** nearly 500 feet in height, affording a fine view of the Avon Valley. About half a mile from the hill, approached by keeping always to the left along a winding lane, is—

Englishcombe,

a picturesque village, once the residence of Saxon kings. The manor was a seat of De Gournay, who took a prominent part in the murder of Edward II. On the accession of this king's son, De Gournay was captured and executed. His castle at Englishcombe was levelled, and the site is now only distinguished by a fosse in the field called Culverhayes. The estates were transferred to the Duchy of Cornwall, the Prince of Wales, as Duke of Cornwall, being now lord of the manor. The **Church** has a Norman door, and there are two Norman pillars in the tower. An antiquarian relic in this interesting spot is a Tithe Barn, built of stones from the castle.

In a field to the west of the church may be seen traces of the **Wansdyke**, a wall of earth with a ditch on each side, extending from the Thames, in Wiltshire, to the Severn at Portishead. Its origin is a favourite subject of discussion among antiquaries; but the lamp of conjecture is the only light that has as yet been thrown upon its history. The consensus of opinion regards it as a boundary thrown up by British tribes for protection. Those who retrace their steps to the tramway route will see another part of the Wansdyke at the rear of the Union Workhouse.

From Englishcombe walk back to Odd Down, and a few yards beyond the Workhouse turn to the left for *Glasshouse Farm*, the end of the 2*d*. tramway stage.

Glasshouse Farm to Combe Down.

The fare is 1*d*. and the route runs along the top of the Down to Combe Down village. From the top of the car, on a clear day, may be distinctly seen in one direction Bath and Bristol; and in the other, the **White Horse**, the famous cutting on the slope of the Wiltshire Downs. This object formed the subject of the story, *The Scouring of the White Horse*, by Thomas Hughes, of *Tom Brown* fame. The tramway route, passing through **Combe Down** village, terminates at the Convalescent Home, and is close to—

Prior Park,

which owes its name to having been a possession of the Priors of Bath. Its special interest now is due to its having been for many years the residence of Ralph Allen.

Ralph Allen, the son of a Cornish innkeeper, gained the favour, when a clerk at the Bath Post Office, of Marshal Wade, commander of the Western District early in the eighteenth century. The story goes that Allen, from an examination of suspicious letters, revealed to the Marshal details of an intended Jacobite rising, and was rewarded with the postmastership of Bath. By his postal reforms he amassed a fortune, which he increased by making known the merits of freestone hewn from the quarries on his estate.

Before Allen's time "Bath stone" was but little used; and part of his object in erecting the mansion at Prior Park was to display the virtues of the stone. In 1742 Allen became Mayor of Bath, the activity he threw into the management of the city leading to the publication of a caricature, *The One-headed Corporation.*

Famous people visited Allen at Prior Park, prominent among them being William Pitt, afterwards Earl of Chatham, the Princess Amelia, Pope, Fielding, Richardson and Warburton. It was through Allen's influence that Pitt was, for several years, one of the representatives of Bath in the House of Commons. Pope finished at Prior Park his *Dunciad*; and ten years later, in the Epilogue to the *Satires*, thus referred to the unobtrusive, charitable qualities of his host—

> "Let humble Allen with an awkward shame
> Do good by stealth and blush to find it fame."

A secluded lane, connecting Perrymead with Combe Down, is known as **Pope's Walk.**

Warburton, afterwards Bishop of Gloucester, a rather quarrelsome and arrogant divine, remembered for his theological works, married Allen's favourite niece, and eventually occupied Prior Park. Warburton won Pope's friendship for his defence of the *Essay on Man* against the attacks of theologians, and the poet gratefully bequeathed to his defender half of his library and the copyright of many of his poems.

Prior Park Mansion,

approached by the last turning to the left before the Combe Down terminus of the tram route is reached, was completed in 1742, so far as the central part of the building is concerned, by the architect Wood. The Corinthian portico of six columns was considered at the time of its erection the most beautiful example of its kind in the kingdom. The length of the frontage, including the wings subsequently added, is 1,300 feet. The mansion, for many years used as a Roman Catholic College, is now empty. Tickets for viewing Prior Park may be obtained (*price* 1s.) at the Lodge Gates.

Combe Down,

which is honeycombed with caverns from which freestone has been excavated, is celebrated for the purity and salubrity of its air, and is in consequence the resort of many invalids.

WALKS FROM COMBE DOWN.

The road to the right from the terminus leads to **Monkton Combe,** and by keeping straight on from the terminus—

CLAVERTON—SHAM CASTLE

Claverton

will be reached in a twenty minutes' walk. This is one of the prettiest spots in the Avon Valley. In the **Church** Ralph Allen was buried in 1766, his monument, standing on three steps, being covered by a pyramidal roof supported on each side by three arches. The churchyard contains an interesting memento of the Civil War, for under its west wall were buried three soldiers of the army of the Parliament and one Royalist, who lost their lives in a skirmish near the ferry in 1643. The story goes that while Sir William Basset, lord of the manor, and a party of Royalists of high birth were dining in Claverton Manor House they were disturbed by a cannon ball, fired from Monkton Farleigh Down, making its way into the room. The skirmish which followed heralded the important battle of Lansdown. The Parliamentarians were chased into Batheaston and Bath, and the road to Oxford was opened to the Royal army.

The **Manor House,** on the crest of the hill, contains some of the stones of the older building, erected in 1588, which stood lower down the hill, just above a flight of stone steps still to be seen near the church.

A mile away, and nearer Bath, approached by a path on the right of North Road, is—

Sham Castle,

an appropriately named structure, for it is only a battlemented wall built in 1760 by Ralph Allen to improve the prospect from his town house in North Parade. It stands at a point from which good views of the city may be obtained. From the road below Sham Castle a path leads to the left across Cleveland Walk towards central Bath.

It is a charming walk from the Combe Down terminus to the **Viaduct,** which can be reached by the road to the right, or by keeping straight on from the terminus towards Claverton, and turning down **Brassknocker Hill,** which is just beyond the Statutory Hospital.

Another favourite walk (about two miles) is to **Conkwell.** For this place, take a footpath leading off from the right a little beyond Brassknocker Hill, which leads down to the Aqueduct, cross by the towing path on the left of the Canal, and then climb up to the village through the woods. These woods are famous as a resort for picnic parties.

III. THE G.W.R. STATION TO WESTON.

Fare, 1d.

This and the route to Newton St. Loe are the only tramway services along which the cars do not start from the Guildhall. The city terminus is at the Great Western Station, and the cars run along Dorchester Street and Southgate Street to Kingsmead Square, the most central starting point from the city. The route to Weston lies along the Upper Bristol Road, as far as the *Weston Hotel*. Opposite the hotel is **Locksbrook Cemetery,** the resting place of Mrs. Luke, whose hymn, *I think when I read that sweet story of Old*, known and loved by children all over the English-speaking world, was written when she was travelling on a stage coach between Taunton and Wellington. The direction is then through Combe Park, past the Cricket Ground of the well-known Lansdown Club, to—

Weston,

an ancient parish two miles to the north-west of Bath. Here was born Alphege, first Abbot of Bath, Archbishop of Canterbury, murdered by the Danes in 1012 for refusing to allow his diocese to be taxed to supply his ransom. The **Church,** mainly a modern structure with a Perpendicular tower, contains some interesting memorials of eminent Bath natives and visitors.

From the farther end of Weston a road leads to—

Prospect Stile,

on **Stoke Brow,** at the end of the racecourse, and less than a mile south-west of the pretty village of **North Stoke.** The beautiful views which it commands include Bath and Bristol, Savernake Forest on the east, Salisbury Plain to the south-east, the Mendips, Bristol Channel and Welsh Mountains on the north and west, and the Forest of Dean on the north.

IV. G.W.R. STATION TO NEWTON ST. LOE AND SALTFORD.

Fares.—From the G.W.R. Station to Newbridge Road, 1d.; to Newbridge, 2d.; to Newton St. Loe, 3d.

This route is the same as the Weston route as far as the Weston Hotel, where it branches off down the Newbridge road.

After leaving the suburban villas behind, a pretty view is obtained of the **Twerton Woods** on the left. About three-quarters of a mile from the terminus the route crosses the Avon, and a delightful view is then obtained of the river, with the **Kelston Woods** as a background on the right.

Newton St. Loe is situated on the summit of a hill. The suffix " St. Loe " is the name of a family who anciently possessed the manor. It is now held by the Gore-Langton family. In the " God's acre " of the Church, which was restored and enlarged in 1857, is an ancient cross.

In **Newton Park**, the residence of Earl Temple, great-grandson of Colonel William Gore-Langton, is the fine Norman gateway, with other remains, of a Castle, where King John lived for a time when worried by his barons.

By descending the hill from the church, crossing a stile, and walking westwards for half a mile along the high road, the visitor will reach the farmhouse known as—

Corston Manor,

once a private school in which Robert Southey spent a short and unhappy period of his life. How he was taken by his father to this school, and the pain the lad—only seven years of age—felt at being left amid such strange associations, is described in Southey's *Retrospect*, written after revisiting Corston in his manhood :—

> " Methinks even now the interview I see,—
> The mistress's glad smile, the master's glee ;
> Much of my future happiness they said,
> Much of the easy life the scholars led,
> Of spacious playground and of wholesome air,
> The best instruction and the tenderest care ;
> And when I followed to the garden-door
> My father, till through tears I saw no more,
> How civilly they sooth'd my parting pain,
> And never did they speak so civilly again."

The tramway is continued for two miles beyond Newton St. Loe to **Saltford**, pleasantly situated in the Avon valley. It is a favourite reach for boating, and here are held the regattas jointly arranged by the rowing clubs of Bath and Bristol.

V. THE GUILDHALL TO TWERTON.

Fare, 1d.

The cars run *via* Southgate Street over the Old Bridge, and along Lower Bristol Road, a populous district chiefly composed of factories and cottages. The route terminates just beyond Twerton railway station.

Twerton.

The **Church** is a modern structure on the site of two earlier buildings, of which a Norman doorway and font, and the Perpendicular tower, are still preserved. In the second house of a row of buildings called Fielding's Terrace, Henry Fielding lived for a time, and wrote several chapters of *Tom Jones*. The parish is chiefly inhabited by workpeople employed in the local cloth factory.

Close to the church, the turning to the right must be taken, and in about three-quarters of a mile the road crosses a tributary of the Avon. Another turning to the right, near the stream, leads to Newton St. Loe.

VI. THE GUILDHALL TO OLDFIELD PARK.

Fare, 1d.

Owing to a low railway bridge crossing the route, it is necessary to use only single-deckers cars. They take the same route as the Twerton cars as far as what is known as the *Green Tree* ; there they branch off on the left to the populous and hilly district of **Oldfield Park**.

From the end of this route, **Englishcombe** is little more than a mile distant. There is another pleasant walk to **Sladebrook** and **Rush Hill**, less than a mile away, and reached by turning to the right at the end of Bath Lane, and taking the first turning to the left.

MOTOR 'BUS ROUTES.

BATHFORD TO BOX.

Fare.—From Guildhall, Bath, tramcar and motor 'bus inclusive, 6d.

Bathford (p. 97) is 3 miles from Bath. Three miles farther along the main road is **Box**, famous for the *St. Aldhelm's Quarries* of Bath stone, and for its tunnel, 1¾ miles in length, the construction of which cost the lives of a hundred men and half a million of money. The strata through which it was cut are the *Great Oolite* (Bath Stone), *Fuller's Earth*, *Inferior Oolite*, *Blue Marl* and *Lias Limestone*.

About midway between Bathford and Box will be seen on the left the classic frontage of **Shockerwick House**, built by the elder Wood for a prosperous carrier, named Wiltshire, a good friend to Gainsborough. It was the custom of the carrier to make no charge for the conveyance to London of the pictures painted by the great artist in Bath. In return Gainsborough forced his friend to accept some of his finest works, such as the *Parish Clerk* and the *Harvest Wagon*, afterwards secured by the National Gallery. It was while visiting Shockerwick House to see these pictures that Pitt heard the news of Napoleon's victory at Austerlitz.

Box Church, originally built early in the thirteenth century, restored in 1713, and more recently enlarged, has an embattled tower, with Perpendicular spire, supported by Early English arches. Other parts of the building are Early English and Decorated. The curious moulding of the arches between the nave and north aisle should be noticed.

Box is the burial-place of Mrs. Bowdler, a writer of repute in her time, and mother of the editor of the *Family Shakespeare*, a work which introduced the word " bowdlerised " into the language. Another literary name connected with the village is that of Coleridge, who lodged at a grocer's shop until he discovered that a barrel of gunpowder was stored beneath his room.

A mile north of Box is **Ditteridge Church,** with Norman nave, chancel and south porch, dedicated to St. Christopher. During the restoration in 1857 a mural painting was discovered of St. Christopher carrying the Infant Christ over a stream, and St. Michael weighing souls. At a short distance from Box is **Cheney Court,** a Tudor mansion. One and a half miles south-east of the village is **Chapel Plaster,** in the fifteenth century a wayside chapel for pilgrims from Malmesbury to Glastonbury ; in the eighteenth century the haunt of a highwayman named Baxter, who was hanged on Claverton Down ; afterwards an outhouse to an inn ; and now restored to sacred uses.

TO CORSHAM AND CHIPPENHAM.

Fares.—From the Guildhall, Bath, tramcar and motor 'bus inclusive, to Corsham, 9d. ; to Chippenham, 1s. 1d.

Corsham, an interesting little town, 2 miles from Box, contains a fine Church with Norman nave arcades, Early English tower and Perpendicular chancel. Another object of interest is—

Corsham Court,

the seat of Lord Methuen. The south front is a splendid specimen of Elizabethan architecture, but the house is most famous for its collection of paintings, one of the finest in the West. Its value is computed to be more than a quarter of a million sterling. *Particulars as to visiting days and arrangements for admission may be obtained at the booksellers, hotels or livery stables.*)

Close to the entrance gates of the Court are the **Almshouses,** founded in 1668 by Lady Hungerford, widow of a former owner of Corsham Court.

The motor 'bus route is continued for 4½ miles beyond Corsham to **Chippenham,** an old market town, once one of the most important centres of the Wiltshire cloth industry, which has declined since the introduction of machinery. A balustraded bridge of many arches crosses the Avon at Chippenham. Three miles away is **Bowood,** the seat of the Marquis of Lansdowne.

BATHFORD TO LACOCK.

Fare.—From the Guildhall, Bath, 1s.

From Bathford, motor 'buses run to **Lacock Abbey,** to which visitors are admitted at a small fee. The imposing remains consist of the domestic buildings of an Augustine Nunnery founded in 1232, and present a most interesting example of the ancient dignity of a conventual establishment. Lacock village, with its many fifteenth and sixteenth century houses, is described as " unique in Wiltshire and not easily matched in England."

BATHFORD TO BRADFORD-ON-AVON AND TROWBRIDGE.

Fares.—From Guildhall, Bath, tramcar and motor 'bus inclusive : to Bradford, 9d. ; to Trowbridge, 1s.

There are some fine views along this route, particularly of the **Limpley Stoke Valley,** the picturesque village of Claverton, and the prospect from Farley Wick, extending towards the south-east from a height of nearly 500 feet to the **White Horse** cut on the slope of the chalk downs at Westbury.

The picturesque town of **Bradford,** built on the steep slope of the riverside hill, and once a more important centre of woollen manufacture than it is now, is about 6 miles from Bathford. Cloth has been made here from a very early period, but, until 1659, the produce was chiefly of a coarse kind resembling drugget. In that year Paul Methuen, of Corsham Court, introduced Flemish weavers for the manufacture of finer cloth, and the trade rapidly increased and extended to the surrounding towns and villages. The part of the town, the west end of Church Street, where the immigrants lived, is still called *Dutch Barton*.

Holy Trinity Church, built in the twelfth century, was restored in 1865–7, and contains Norman work in the south wall of the nave and the west end of the chancel.

The most interesting building in the town is the **Saxon Church,** close to Holy Trinity Church. It was built early in the eighth century by Aldhelm, Bishop of Sherborne, and dedicated to St. Lawrence ; and there can be no question that it is the most ancient unaltered church in England. The nave is 24 feet long, and the chancel 13 feet. The building had been used as a cottage and a free school, and was fast falling into ruin when it was rescued and restored, in the latter half of the nineteenth century, by the efforts of a vicar of Holy Trinity.

In the centre of the town is a very ancient **Bridge,** with nine arches, having over one of the piers a curious structure which has been in turns a chapel, a lock-up, a toolhouse, and an ammunition store for Territorials.

Other places of interest in Bradford are the **Tithe Barn,** with its gabled doorways and buttressed walls of the fifteenth century, situated in *Barton Farm*, on the station side of the river ; and the **Hall,** reached from the Market Place by the quaint Shambles and Silver Street. When an example of Elizabethan domestic architecture was required for the Paris Exposition of 1900, this remarkably beautiful building was chosen as the model.

Two and a half miles from Bradford is the **Winsley Sanatorium,** serving the counties of Wilts, Gloucester and Somerset.

To **Trowbridge** is a twenty minutes' run by motor 'bus from Bradford. In the chancel of the Parish Church is buried the poet Crabbe, Rector of Trowbridge for eighteen years. The town, the birthplace of Sir Isaac Pitman, has a population of over 11,000. It was once a more thriving centre than now for the manufacture of West of England cloth.

BATH TO NORTON ST. PHILIP AND FROME.

Fares.—From Guildhall, Bath, inclusive of tramcar and motor 'bus : to Norton St. Philip, 7d. ; to Frome, 1s. 1d.

The route is by Combe Down tramcar as far as Glasshouse

TOURS FROM BATH

Farm ; thence by motor 'bus through the picturesque **Midford Valley**, and past the village of **Hinton Charterhouse.**

TO RADSTOCK AND MIDSOMER NORTON.

Fares.—From Guildhall, Bath, inclusive of tramcar and motor 'bus : to Radstock, 10*d.* ; to Midsomer Norton, 11*d.*

Radstock is the centre of a colliery district ; **Midsomer Norton,** two miles beyond, is pleasantly set in a wooded valley. The motor 'bus route is from Glasshouse Farm.

TO PAULTON.

Fare.—From Guildhall, Bath, 11*d.*

The route is by tramcar to Newton St. Loe ; thence by motor 'bus along a road affording fine views of the Mendips.

BATH TO LANSDOWN HILL.

Motor 'buses run from Bath to the top of Lansdown Hill and the Lansdown Golf Links ; to Hamilton Road, 3*d.* ; to Hamilton House, 4*d.*

PLEASURE TOURS BY MOTOR CHAR-À-BANC.

To **Lansdown Battle Field.**—A motor 'bus leaves the Guildhall at 11.15 and 3 p.m. for the famous battlefield. Return fare, 1*s.*

I. To **Castle Combe** *viâ* Bannerdown, returning *viâ* Yatton Keynell, leaving the Guildhall at 2.30. An afternoon trip through some of the most charming scenery in the district.

II. To **Farleigh Castle** and **Bradford-on-Avon.** Morning and afternoon tours, visiting the ruins of Farleigh Castle and the numerous historic buildings at Bradford-on-Avon, including the Saxon Church.

III. To **Cheddar, Glastonbury** and **Wells.** From the Guildhall at 10 a.m. The route is *viâ* Marksbury and West Harptree to Cheddar, where ample time is allowed for lunch and a visit to the caves. Return *viâ* Glastonbury and Wells.

IV. To **Salisbury** and **Stonehenge.** Out *viâ* Limpley Stoke Valley, Beckington, Warminster and Heytesbury

CHAR-A-BANC TOURS

to Salisbury (stay about two hours) then *via* Amesbury to Stonehenge, returning *via* Shrewton, West Lavington, Edington, Steeple Ashton and Hilperton. Leave Guildhall 10 a.m.

V. To **Marlborough** and **Savernake Forest.** Out *via* Corsham, Lacock, Calne, Cherhill and Avebury to Marlborough; round Savernake Forest, returning *via* Marlborough, Beckhampton, Hilperton and Staverton. Leave Guildhall 10 a.m.

VI. To **Gloucester** and **Berkeley Castle.** Leave Guildhall 10 a.m. A tour of great historic interest combined with exquisite scenery.

VII. To **Clevedon** and **Portishead,** *via* Keynsham, across the Clifton Suspension Bridge, through Failand and Portbury to Portishead and Clevedon, returning *via* Yatton, Brockley Combe, Chew Magna and Stanton Drew. A halt is made at each point. Leave Guildhall at 10 a.m.

VIII. To **Cheltenham** and the **Seven Springs.** Leave Guildhall at 10 a.m. Out *via* Gloucester Road, Nailsworth, Stroud and Painswick to Cheltenham (stay 1¼ hours). Return *via* Seven Springs (the source of the Thames),Cirencester, Malmesbury and Chippenham.

Some of these tours are run at least once a week during the season. Full particulars can be obtained and seats booked at the Company's Booking Office at 10, Old Bond Street, and 31, Southgate Street, also at the Pump Room Enquiry Office and the hotels.

BATH ROWING CLUB REGATTA : WATCHING FOR THE BOATS.

A MEET OF THE SOUTH-WEST WILTS FOXHOUNDS.

THE BATH STONE QUARRIES.

IN the heart of the lofty and wide-spreading uplands amid which the city of Bath nestles, are mines and quarries which regularly send out their treasures of the great Oolite, or freestone, formation, to be employed in the erection of " all sorts and conditions " of buildings—churches and palaces, theatres and public halls, schools, institutes and railway stations.

That " Bath Stone," as the material is called, is so durable as to be classed as " time-defying," is shown in the Roman remains at Bath, hewn from quarries in the neighbourhood, and preserving to this day the clearly marked cuttings in ornaments, figures and letters, fashioned by the skilled artist nearly twenty centuries ago. Testimony almost as remarkable is afforded by the Saxon Church at Bradford and the venerable Abbey at Malmesbury, both built of stone cut from the extensive and historic quarry at Box. It is nearly 1,100 years since Malmesbury Abbey was founded ; and when the structure was restored in recent years, it was to the same Box quarry that the builders came for their material—a remarkable instance of business continuity.

Among other structures made of Bath Stone may be mentioned the stately and historic seat of Longleat ; the Iron Duke's residence, Apsley House, in Piccadilly ; Spurgeon's Tabernacle, and the City Temple ; while the whole of beautiful Bath, clad as in a soft grey mantle, remains in ever-present witness of the virtues of the stone hewn from the green-covered uplands that look so smilingly down upon the fair city to which they gave birth.

A typical stone mine is that at Monk's Park, Corsham, one of many belonging to the great organization of stone merchants known as the *Bath Stone Firms, Limited.* Monk's Park stone is an Oolitic of the best quality, very strong, and so close and compact in grain that the finest details can be cut into it effectively. It is found at depths varying from 100 to 120 feet, sandwiched between masses of ragstone, the upper portion of which, as the excavations proceed, form the ceiling, and the lower bed the floor of the mine. Although they penetrate for miles beneath the ground, the mines have so healthy an atmosphere that the workmen are remarkable for their sturdy and robust appearance.

As a rule, the blocks of stone do not exceed seven tons in weight, but some have been cut weighing as many as ten tons, notably those supplied to India ; for to the distant East, as well as to South Africa, has the fame of Bath Stone penetrated. When the blocks are drawn to the surface they are stacked all through the spring and summer, and when completely dried by exposure to sun and breeze are for ever impervious to rain, or even to damp,

Visitors descend into **Monk's Park Quarry** through what is called the " heading," or opening, down a long flight of steps, at the bottom of which they are supplied with the necessary oil lamps fixed to a piece of flat wood, the same means of light used by the workmen.

Besides this mine there are many similar workings, such as the ancient **Box Quarry**, already mentioned in connection with the building of Malmesbury Abbey ; and having taken so important a part in religious work, the quarry's claim to possess a *Cathedral* of its own will be accepted with due reverence. This stately title was originally given by the workmen to the now disused portions of the workings which were formerly entered from the top. The name, fanciful but not far-fetched, was suggested by the general shape of that part of the quarry. Here we have a " nave " 80 feet in height, two small openings to serve as " transepts," and beyond a continuation to serve as a " choir."

The Box workings extend for miles ; " a marvellous maze," says a recent writer, " growing year after year, through which the miners, or quarreymen, nevertheless find their way, as their forbears did before them, as easily and as confidently as Londoners do through their puzzling street windings and turnings."

Close to the old village of Pickwick, near Corsham, there is another well-known mine, called the **Hartham Park Quarry.**

It may here be stated that visitors are made welcome at the mines, and supplied with lights as well as guides to point the way through the otherwise untrackable mazes that honeycomb the breezy uplands around Bath.

Are we down-hearted? No-o-o! A WW1 morale-boosting magic lantern slide

An electric tram

Great Pulteney Street

Hedgemead Park

Milsom Street (above, below and next page)

Bathampton Ferry

Southgate Place

Pulteney Bridge

Southgate Street

Stall Street

Castle Combe (above, below and next page)

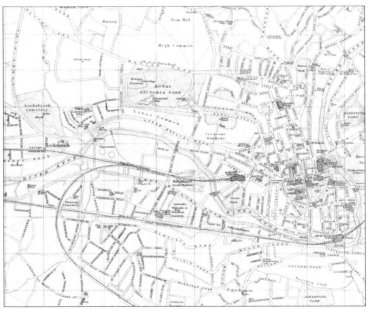

City centre map from the 1917 guide-book

Andrew Gill: I have collected early photographs and optical antiques for over forty years. I am a professional 'magic lantern' showman presenting lantern slide shows and giving talks on Victorian optical entertainments for museums, festivals, special interest groups and universities.

For information about magic lanterns and slides and to contact me, please visit my website **Magic Lantern World** at www.magiclanternist.com

I have published historical booklets and photo albums on the subjects below. They are available from amazon, some as printed books, some as e-books, many in both formats. To see them all and 'look inside', simply search for one of my titles, then click the 'Andrew Gill' link. Alternatively, go to the 'My photo-history booklets' page on my website (see above) and click on the link.

Historical travel guides
New York
Jersey in 1921
Norwich in 1880
Doon the Watter
Liverpool in 1886
Nottingham in 1899
Bournemouth in 1914
Great Yarmouth in 1880
Victorian Walks in Surrey
The Way We Were: Bath
A Victorian Visit to Brighton
A Victorian Visit to Hastings
A Victorian Visit to Falmouth
Newcastle upon Tyne in 1903
Victorian and Edwardian York
The Way We Were: Llandudno
Doncaster: The Way We Were

Victorian and Edwardian Leeds
The Way We Were: Manchester
Victorian and Edwardian Bradford
Victorian and Edwardian Sheffield
A Victorian Visit to Fowey and Looe
A Victorian Visit to Peel, Isle of Man
The Way We Were: The Lake District
Lechlade to Oxford by Canoe in 1875
Guernsey, Sark and Alderney in 1921
East Devon through the Magic Lantern
The River Thames from Source to Sea
North Devon through the Magic Lantern
A Victorian Visit to Ramsey, Isle of Man
A Victorian Visit to Douglas, Isle of Man
Victorian Totnes through the Magic Lantern
Victorian Whitby through the Magic Lantern
Victorian London through the Magic Lantern
St. Ives through the Victorian Magic Lantern
Victorian Torquay through the Magic Lantern
Victorian Glasgow through the Magic Lantern
The Way We Were: Wakefield and Dewsbury
The Way We Were: Hebden Bridge to Halifax
Victorian Scarborough through the Magic Lantern
The Way We Were: Hull and the surrounding area
The Way We Were: Harrogate and Knaresborough
A Victorian Tour of North Wales: Rhyl to Llandudno
A Victorian Visit to Lewes and the surrounding area
The Isle of Man through the Victorian Magic Lantern
A Victorian Visit to Helston and the Lizard Peninsula
A Victorian Railway Journey from Plymouth to Padstow
A Victorian Visit to Barmouth and the Surrounding Area
A Victorian Visit to Malton, Pickering and Castle Howard
A Victorian Visit to Eastbourne and the surrounding area
A Victorian Visit to Aberystwyth and the Surrounding Area
A Victorian Visit to Castletown, Port St. Mary and Port Erin
Penzance and Newlyn through the Victorian Magic Lantern
A Victorian Journey to Snowdonia, Caernarfon and Pwllheli
Victorian Brixham and Dartmouth through the Magic Lantern
Victorian Plymouth and Devonport through the Magic Lantern
A Victorian Tour of North Wales: Conwy to Caernarfon via Anglesey
Dawlish, Teignmouth and Newton Abbot through the Victorian Magic
Lantern
Staithes, Runswick and Robin Hood's Bay through the Magic Lantern
A Victorian Visit to Cornwall: Morwenstow to Tintagel via Kilkhampton,
Bude, Boscastle and Bossiney

Other historical topics
Sarah Jane's Victorian Tour of Scotland
The River Tyne through the Magic Lantern
The 1907 Wrench Cinematograph Catalogue
Victorian Street Life through the Magic Lantern
The First World War through the Magic Lantern
Ballyclare May Fair through the Victorian Magic Lantern
The Story of Burnley's Trams through the Magic Lantern

The Franco-British 'White City' London Exhibition of 1908
The 1907 Wrench 'Optical and Science Lanterns' Catalogue
How They Built the Forth Railway Bridge: A Victorian Magic Lantern Show

Walking Books
Victorian Edinburgh Walks
Victorian Rossendale Walks
More Victorian Rossendale Walks
Victorian Walks on the Isle of Wight (Book 1)
Victorian Walks on the Isle of Wight (Book 2)
Victorian Rossendale Walks: The End of an Era

Historical photo albums (just photos)
The Way We Were: Suffolk
Norwich: The Way We Were
Sheffield: The Way We Were
The Way We Were: Somerset
Fife through the Magic Lantern
York through the Magic Lantern
Rossendale: The Way We Were
The Way We Were: Lincolnshire
The Way We Were: Cumberland
Burnley through the Magic Lantern
Oban to the Hebrides and St. Kilda
Tasmania through the Magic Lantern
Swaledale through the Magic Lantern
Llandudno through the Magic Lantern
Birmingham through the Magic Lantern
Penzance, Newlyn and the Isles of Scilly
Great Yarmouth through the Magic Lantern
Ancient Baalbec through the Magic Lantern
The Isle of Skye through the Magic Lantern
Ancient Palmyra through the Magic Lantern
The Kentish Coast from Whitstable to Hythe
New South Wales through the Magic Lantern
From Glasgow to Rothesay by paddle steamer
Victorian Childhood through the Magic Lantern
The Way We Were: Yorkshire Railway Stations
Southampton, Portsmouth and the Great Liners
Newcastle upon Tyne through the Magic Lantern
Egypt's Ancient Monuments through the Magic Lantern
The Way We Were: Birkenhead, Port Sunlight and the Wirral
Ancient Egypt, Baalbec and Palmyra through the Magic Lantern

Printed in Great Britain
by Amazon

57065813R00078